JESUS SPEAKS

THE STUDY GUIDE

GLENDA GREEN

Spiritis

Published by: Spiritis Publishing
P.O. Box 1744, Aransas Pass, TX 78335
www.lovewithoutend.com (1-888-453-6324)

Cover painting: *First Light*, a spiritual portrait of Jesus Christ.
©Glenda Green, 1998.
Back Cover painting: *"Jeshua,"* ©Glenda Green, 2006.

Printed in the United States of America

Your Guide

to

Love Without End

Dedication

This Study Guide is dedicated to all those who
carried the torch in the early years by their own
devotion and resources, to see that
"Love Without End, Jesus Speaks" was taught to anyone
who needed introduction or assistance.
To all those who formed study groups,
who gave public presentations,
or took loving initiative
of any kind assisting others to
understand these messages of Jesus.

Table of Contents

Introduction.. 1
Lesson 1.. 9
Lesson 2.. 21
Lesson 3.. 29
Lesson 4.. 40
Lesson 5.. 53
Lesson 6.. 63
Lesson 7.. 71
Lesson 8.. 83
Lesson 9.. 89
Lesson 10....................................... 97
Lesson 11....................................... 103
Lesson 12....................................... 109
Lesson 13....................................... 121
Lesson 14....................................... 133
Lesson 15....................................... 143
Summation....................................... 153

Introduction

Activate Christ Presence Within

The goal of this Study Guide is to help readers of "*Love Without End, Jesus Speaks*" comprehend its messages more fully, while finding its relevance to their own spiritual growth and enlightenment. This book is not meant to be read on its own, but as a companion to the book it guides you through. I don't even suggest that you use the study guide your first time through "*Love Without End,*" which is a warm and easy read, even though a long one. It was written at the level of personal experience with great care to be understandable and beneficial to any reader.

This is why, for seventeen years, it did not occur to me that a companion book for study assistance was necessary. In seminars and webinars we took the study deeper, because the book does present some rather sophisticated explanations about life, which provide a whole new exploration for 21st century students of Jesus' teachings. These would, of course, had no place in the context of his world two thousand years ago.

However, what I began to realize as I worked with students over the last two decades, is the real book they were trying to uncover is the one inside themselves. "*Love Without End*" is only a place to begin, a doorway to walk through, if you will. Anyone who has read "*Love*

Without End" more than once, with underlined passages on every page and many of them dog-eared is ready for the Study Guide. Your next step is to join the messages in "Love Without End" to your own book of life.

Any subject that is truly alive, or has value to life, causes us to grow. As we expand our awareness and our senses we see and hear more. Jesus' immortal admonition to the Apostles was, "I speak to all who have the ears to hear and the eyes to see." Today, we have new eyes and new ears. This Study Guide is to help you get the most out of what you see and hear on the pages of *"Love Without End, Jesus Speaks."*

We will begin with the dedication:

> *Our Father who is innocent and pure,*
> *Holy is your name.*
> *May love be seen as all that is.*
> *May earth be seen as heaven is.*
> *Nourish this day with your bountiful supply,*
> *And allow us to receive as we give that right to others.*
> *Restore us from the perils of illusion,*
> *And renew our perception of truth.*
> *For truth is the kingdom, and love is the power,*
> *And Yours is the glory forever.*

This prayer was Jesus' gift to me as I neared completion of the manuscript. I was actually in prayer, asking for any final thoughts or summation of thoughts for his messages, when the words of this prayer spilled out from my heart and mouth with such clarity that I opened my eyes and quickly transcribed them. In the simplest language, in the purest distillation of the message, this prayer is the summation of *"Love Without End."* When I heard these words, I knew the book was finished. By taking this prayer to heart you are attuning your consciousness to the ultimate integration of its meaning.

This Study Guide was expressly designed for the third edition (and later editions) of the book. However, it will work equally well for earlier editions (those characterized by Parts I and II) as long as its reader makes one small adjustment. You will have to read all of Part I as your equivalent to Chapter 1 in the Study Guide. After that the editions are closely similar.

The original book is read around the world in seven languages. Its readers are in all countries, and all ages from young people starting out to retired individuals summarizing their life. It's read by thousands of people whose jobs are rather ordinary, but they want to have extraordinary lives, all the way to university professors, PhD physicists, PhD psychologists, Priests, Medical Doctors, celebrities, and public officials. All it takes from anyone are fresh eyes, fresh ears, and a desire to find something amazing within themselves.

Those who do not have reading proficiency or limited vocabularies will need to look up a few words as you go. Always be clear about what you read. If you live such a busy life that "speed reading" is the only way to take in a new book, you will need to be aware that quick scanning builds 'concept generalities.' At some point you will want to break down those generalities into particulars that you can absorb and integrate into your personal reality. "Generalities" are also susceptible to being compiled with old beliefs and assumptions that may need to be reexamined. This study guide will help all levels of readers find their way to making this book their own path of wisdom.

The Guide will address many questions that have come up through the years from many readers. Hopefully, it will help future readers gain a more authentic and direct understanding of Jesus' messages. As his messages are clarified, it is my greatest hope that you will also expand in faith, conviction, compassion, and wisdom to access the presence of Christ within yourself.

As other readers will tell you, "Love Without End" is alive and always sensitive to each person's needs and quest for learning. It leads us to grow in our ability to see what we have never seen or heard before, and to find just what we need in present time. It also leads us into community with others seeking the same level of discovery and wisdom.

> The goal of every lesson is to make possible new realizations and insights about both the book **and your own life!**

Each lesson in the Guide will correspond to one chapter in *"Love Without End"* and present questions and suggestions for taking your studies into the highest level of personal comprehension. The Guide will be directed toward expansion of awareness with emphasis more on personal relevance rather than didactic explanations of specific content in the book. The primary goal of this Study Manual is to support you in attaining a fuller, richer, healthier, happier, and more compassionate life.

> Open yourself to the infinite lighted path.
> Find out who you really are
> Find more love, joy, and fulfillment **now.**
> Overcome personal patterns that have attracted hardship and pain.
> Learn simple, powerful principles of the universe that are available to all.
> Experience your own living communion with Christ!
> Learn what Jesus meant when he said
> "All these things you shall do and more."

Each lesson will begin with an essay that focuses on highlights of the correlating chapter. My intent is to remove all the complexity that may have occurred within the book's conversational flow and to bring into clear view the principle teachings and how they may become most relevant to you. Hopefully my own growth in the last 22 years will bring further enhancement in that I too had the same opportunity and challenge of integrating his messages into my personal life.

Following the essay there will be study questions. The purpose of these questions will be to propel you into active dialogue with the messages.

You will need to ask, dig, and retrieve until you have emerged with a pearl of your own wisdom.

Following the study questions will be study exercises. These are only suggestions, and you can tailor each one to your own level of study or accomplishment in life. However, I do suggest that you spend a comparable amount of time, thought, and effort on activating the principles into your flow of experience.

In some lessons there will be a meditation and prayer, in those cases where I feel only inner work can complete and fulfill the revelation.

Finally, you will need to purchase a notebook that can be your working journal. I also recommend placing lesson tabs in your journal for ease of reference, and to make a place that come ahead of the curve as well as reflections back on earlier chapters. You will probably cross-reference from one lesson to another many times. Each lesson in your Guide will have ample space at the end for notes and observations, although I think you may want to keep your flow of thoughts in your working journal and then add the "Jewels" of realization to your Study Guide to make your own insights and discoveries a permanent part of the Guide.

Two thousand years ago when Jesus set forth his teachings, which have since become the foundation of Christianity, he did not intend for anyone to become dependent on external authority, which can then limit one's self confidence in spirit. Instead, he meant for us to discover our internal authority given by God, which allows us to recognize the Word and ultimately even BE the Word. To that end, he promised that we would receive a Counselor in Spirit for our ultimate attainment. The Counselor, which is the Holy Spirit, was referred to by Paul more than once as 'the presence of Christ Within, the hope of glory'. (Colossians 1:27)

Jesus said: 'If you continue in my word...you shall know the truth and the truth shall set you free.' (John 8:31-32) This principle of personal enlightenment, freedom, and integrity is no less true with "Love Without End." One constant you can count on with regard to any higher teaching is this: If it IS TRUE it will set you free! In so doing, it will restore your personal integrity and right relationship with the Creator.

If left to your own, you could very easily sit in an easy chair and ponder the messages in *"Love Without End,"* trying to objectify them, and in so doing pushing them away from what is real for you. Or you could take the general concepts and combine them with old ideas and beliefs that are more comfortable to retain. Either way would be less than optimum, since the power of these messages is to ignite your own awareness of all that are being revealed to you now.

This is the path of realizing and accepting the presence of The Christ within, which is your own birthright and your own original state of being. Otherwise, it could not be said that in our innocence we were created in the image of God!

Now, before we proceed, I would like to offer some considerations about the names of Christ, which do vary in my other books. Let's begin with Christ, which is the Greek variant of Messiah, and Immanuel is another appropriate designation for him in that it also means the anointed one. However, he also had a personal name. In his native language of Aramaic it was Jeshua, and Jehoshua in Hebrew. At the time of his first visitations to me I only knew him as Jesus, which is the name I learned in church and read in English translations of the Bible. Because of all I would later learn about how his various names were intertwined with theology and doctrine, I came to prefer the simple grace of his personal name Jeshua. My later books would reflect that change of preference. However, respecting that *"Love Without End, Jesus Speaks"* was written at the time when I called him Jesus, and that is the source and reason for this study guide, we will remain consistent in this book with the name Jesus. After all, a rose is a rose, and he is **who he is** regardless of what name we choose.

> What is often difficult to see on our own, is that higher wisdom has always been with us. We have simply forgotten how to find it.

After countless generations, we are still seeking the Holy Grail, still searching for the Paradise that was lost.   We were born originally of

6

spirit, and we will be born again to that state of authentic self when we realize who and what we are. The more aware we are of the indwelling spirit, the greater the inflow of spiritual energy and power into our hearts and minds. Even as you have slept or engaged in illusions of separation, a higher consciousness has been growing inside you. Now it is time to awaken and discover that you ARE life, light, and the power of God residing in physical form.

It is to this fact that Jesus was referring when he said: 'Anyone believing in me shall do the same miracles I have done, and even greater ones'. (John 14:12) In that same vein he said to me, 'All things can be yours if you will only emulate the Christ presence I have revealed and awaken to your true relationship with God'.

'I am the light of the world; he that follows me shall not walk in darkness, but shall have the light of life.'(John 8:12) It is from this illumined consciousness that we are born again into a state of knowing from which we can say... 'Father, honor me with the glory that I knew with You before the world was made.'(John 17:5)

I promise this is not beyond your grasp. If anything, you have undershot your grasp... until now! Let the love, truth, and wisdom of Jesus' words in *"Love Without End,"* propel you into your true relationship with God and the universe. Let the harmonic resonance of your heart seeking the love of God and others, bring you to enlightenment

Welcome to the deeper study of *"Love Without End, Jesus Speaks."* May you find truth, love, and freedom, as well as the sunlit places of your own heaven within.

Glenda Green
May 6, 2015

My Personal Notes and Comments

Lesson 1

Let There Be Light

There are three major themes in Chapter One, and it is essential that you grasp these to prepare yourself for all the following lessons.

1. The tendency of human ego (and its defenses) is to see both worldly future and our higher potential as being limited to its own level of experience.

2. The multi-dimensional nature of our universe, which informs our normal senses and also conveys information far beyond them.

3. The supremacy of faith, which brings us greater riches, wisdom, and power than the mind can even conceive. Yet it requires the lesson of surrender before we can be initiated into its miraculous nature.

All of these themes are interconnected in one great lesson, and that will be our primary focus in this chapter. That lesson is surrender. Perhaps our greatest obstacle is misunderstanding of what this means, so let's deal with that first.

Most often we regard surrender as a prelude to defeat. Worse than that, we view surrender as a concession to dominant forces, to give up, relinquish our dreams, or to become a less conspicuous target for opposition. Worst of all, most of us have at least one sickening experience of propitiating to an adversary to prevent defeat. With all these negative associations about surrender, how can we ever see it as a way to enlightenment and freedom? How can we know that we are surrendering to a higher force?

Let's begin with a very neutral examination of surrender. What I learned from Jesus is that a call to surrender is a kind of "signal" to stop resisting something that is really incontestable. Perhaps it's something I don't like, that I dread, or don't understand. It could be as innocent as a child resisting bedtime; or, as understandable as someone having a toothache and trying everything else before giving in to a dental appointment. Then, of course, there's the classic resistance to defeat, but it is not surrender that **causes** the defeat! Surrender is actually a safety signal that tells a person to STOP dangerous activity, or at least to stop wasting energy on actions or attitudes that will inevitably not pay off. Since this signal rings louder in "losing" situations, we have naturally developed associations between surrender and loss.

> In the most neutral sense, surrender is a message to **stop** wasting energy on **any** action or attitude, which will inevitably not result bring about a good result!

That is what we need to correct **now**, because we need to consider this: Limiting beliefs and attitudes can be an even greater source of defeat, and they too strike a "signal to surrender" when we need to step outside those boundaries or grow beyond them.

This can apply equally to excess in successful situations as well as pouring too much time and energy into losing ones. **In other words we need to know when to call our wins before they reverse and our losses before they consume us.** For, both wins and losses are just scores in the game, and events in the process. They do not define us, and are not who we REALLY are.

Now, can you see how the fear of surrender, ironically, can steer you directly into defeat, as well as impair your ability to win?

Fear is a life-protecting signal, in the same way that pain is. No one likes pain, but to dread or ignore signals of fear and pain when they happen is the same as removing the brakes from your automobile. How can you change directions if you can't slow down first or take precautions on a dangerous road?

Such was the case with me in 1991. Fear of surrender was getting in the way of my willingness to take on Jesus' commission. My devotion to ordinary logic, justified behavior, and old familiar patterns of reality had established a wide array of limiting beliefs. I did not yet recognize them as limiting or even as beliefs. I did not know how much less I had settled for than was truly possible. I had established ordinary experience as the standard for my life expectations...not even realizing that was just a convenient belief!

It is amazing how much I had assumed about life without ever examining my presumptions clearly and with consideration for other alternatives. A goldfish in a bowl, looking beyond, does not know that the glass wall of its little environment separates its familiar watery element from a totally different one. The goldfish has just considered its perceptions to be background and never examined them in a broader context, to which it had no access. This is why my surrender was so challenging. What limitation, condition, or resistance did I need to release in surrender?"

Often the demands for surrender are spiritual more than physical or societal. Many analogies have been drawn to express the essence of spiritual surrender. It has sometimes been described as becoming an instrument in the hands of God. Rumi, for example, compared himself to a harp upon which the Divine played wonderful melodies. Other images are more passive. According to Jeanne de Chantal, we might become like an empty container, ready to be filled. For others, surrender means dissolving like a drop that falls into the ocean. For Veronica Giuliani, the soul in a state of ecstasy feels itself transported by waves into an immense sea of love. The most frequent metaphors belong to the biological realm. For Saint Therese of Lisie surrender is like the sleep of a child in its mother's arms.

> What keeps us from total surrender is also the cause of our other troubles in life.

That is our selfish will, originating in the belief that we are separate from everything, and thus act accordingly. This incapacity to let go is the source of hatred, anger, separateness, and the fear of death. We go through life constantly looking for guarantees, endeavoring to control people and circumstances, striving to mold the world to our plans. What a waste of precious time and energy!

> But what if we were to sign a blank check to the universe? What if we fully surrendered? Such an attitude entails courage, generosity, and a degree of truthfulness that enables us to call ourselves into question, risking everything we are. When we do this we are able to see — in the terrifying unknown confronting us — a Will that is infinitely good and wise, and to this Will we can give ourselves without reservation.

Surrendering to Divine Will consists in accepting whatever happens as part of the Divine Plan. This does not absolve **us** from responsibility for making right choices and determinations, or holding onto constructive values. For, these indeed affirm and confirm the love that we are. Our choices are the rudder on the ship which God propels. What it does mean is that God – the highest force of Creation – is always right, even through storms and the illusions of loss. There is a greater plan that puts wind in our sails. The Power to which we have surrendered enters our being and performs a mission we would have been incapable of doing alone, a work of purification and release. It is a hidden, wonderful work that brings not only joy but also at times deep pain. One can do nothing but allow it to have its way and surrender to it in perfect trust. It is infinitely wise, powerful, and ultimately beneficial to souls who place their hope in it without reservation, and who believe with complete faith and unshakeable trust that whatever it does at every moment is for the best.

> Happiness, then, is available here and now. But it is a completely different kind of happiness than anything our minds imagine or conditions of life can supply.

The only time in which surrender is possible is the present. The past of regret or fond memories; or a future full of goals, desires, and anxieties no longer command our lives once we have given ourselves completely to a higher Will. Only the present counts. And we do not strive to change it, because each moment is perfect as it is. The only change is internal: we align our will with what is happening.

This describes my state of joy in 1991, when I finally surrendered to the inevitable opportunity of walking on this high path. I had been holding on tightly, and in my clinging I felt both desire and anxiety. To what was I clinging? **To everything I had**—the sense of existing, a way of life, material goals, and the promise of happiness. In remaining attached to these things I had to struggle, because I always felt in danger of losing what I thought was my heart's desire. **It was a question of hold on, or lose my hold on life.** This 'grasp of life' and struggle to maintain control was partly because of my own being and beliefs, but also because of my habits, expectations, and even cellular programming to stay within a zone of safety the body could also trust.

> Then in a moment of faith, in an instant when I saw beyond ordinary reality, I allowed myself to let go... I flew!

I had no idea what would happen. I abandoned every point of reference. The burden of suspicion and effort I had carried around had vanished. I realized that my life had always been part of some plan and Intelligence far greater than my own, and the weight of my separate, personal identity was lifted. Suddenly I felt a lightness I had never known before. I was at peace.

This was a high moment of surrender for me. And, all of us are familiar with some form of delicious surrender that is possible every day—in sleep, when we yield to the darkness of night and unconsciousness; in laughter, when we momentarily relinquish all inhibitions. Surprising ourselves with our own spontaneity, we forget all our well-rehearsed plans.

Behind every act of genuine surrender lives faith fulfilled; behind every failure to surrender lays confidence betrayed, a wound that will never be forgotten, a fear of disintegration and death.

Surrender refreshes and regenerates. Failure to surrender strains and wearies. Without surrender one becomes hesitant and rigid. Laughter is forced, sleep disturbed, and spontaneity is lost.

Despite all our fears and resistances, the search for surrender is universal. How revitalizing it would be to do away with all care and worry! Deep down we know that such relief is possible — and we desperately long for it. But surrender can be unconscious or conscious, constructive or destructive. Some people let go with joy, while others give up in despair. Some seek release by taking alcohol or drugs, sitting in front of television for hours on end, or listening to loud music. These forms of surrender are full of darkness; they dull and bewilder the heart and soul. All the while they stand in for the not admitted yet longed for desire to experience surrender, perhaps therein is the real hold of our debilitating attachments.

Conscious surrender is the highest surrender, the truest expression of the soul's desire to ascend beyond the worldly contests for survival. It yields to a greater Will, and stems naturally from detachment and devotion. It is the most complete absence of calculation and pretense — an attitude unclouded by preferences, which greets all inner and outer possibilities with openness and generosity. It is this kind of surrender that Jesus taught us.

As you read about my challenge to surrender, consider your own invitations to surrender, and notice how you approach or resist these opportunities. Also, take note of what has happened in the past when you relaxed your resistance to change or accepted more of life.

> Note three instances in your life when surrender paid off in noticeable ways,
>
> What are you resisting most now? What would it cost to surrender? What would be the results?

The second major theme of this chapter is that of opening our perceptions and beliefs to accept many more dimensions of the universe than we had believed were possible. Please note the scientific ideas mentioned in the opening pages of this chapter. These contain prophetic ponderings of many more scientific ideas to come. We are very fortunate to be living at a time when our belief in multiple dimensions of reality is beginning to be borne out by exploratory evidence that is too convincing to disregard.

Nevertheless, this chapter is not about science. It is essentially one of faith. It is not my place to impress my experience, or any beliefs, upon you. It is far better if I can lead you to discover the power within yourself to reveal expanded reality, and this need not be a scientific exploration. It is more important that you explore with your perceptions and your heart to discover dimensions of reality and guidance that exceed your mind's current capacity.

Most people just assume that our three-dimensional reality is much the same for everyone, with different perspectives, and experiences, with many different forms and processes going on.

That seems to be the 'path of least resistance' toward having a consistent and unified explanation of life. But just stop for a moment and consider how many occurrences cannot be explained by a simple 'consistent' reality. Do you have children, grandchildren, pets, or plants in your household? In each case, does it not require a shift in consciousness to 'tune in' to their feelings and needs? Even then, how different it may be from our own! Now, consider your own shifts in consciousness between working, playing, or praying? In each of these realms of consciousness, are there not different packages of energy and whole new worlds of possibility unavailable in the other realms? And, we have not even addressed the realm of miracles!

It is we who have created and believed in limitations of reality. There are many reasons we do that, ranging from conformity, to limited information, to false beliefs, fear, and common laziness. Be mindful, however; **limitations do not originate in the universe. It is we who create them, and it is we who are called to overcome them!**

Rather than focusing on your limitations in this opening part of your study, I would like you to consider your own 'extra perceptions' of life, and consider how you may develop and explore them to find more delight, expansion, and heightened purpose for your life.

The third major theme of this chapter is learning to understand what faith really is and how to find that power within ourselves.

My most vivid recollection of acquiring faith is from the days (and years) when I took *"The Lamb and The Lion"* out to the world, a task for which I was utterly 'unprepared'. I witnessed countless miracles that further challenged my reality, and finally lived through the mutilation of the painting and its miraculous restoration to wholeness.

Unlike what many have assumed, faith is not blind. In fact, it is our **higher sight** that allows us to progress with certainty into a future that has not yet been confirmed by our ordinary senses or experience. Some may say that everything is by faith, even the sun's rising tomorrow. There is certainly some truth to that, but this is not the faith that works miracles, the faith that Jesus taught and confirmed with his life.

Because we are a 'whole' being; and are, by extension, part of a greater 'whole', we have senses that can detect many normally unseen parts of our larger environment. We have learned to limit our focus to the obvious. However, we are aware of unseen factors on other levels of consciousness, if only in our dreams. We ONLY lose this awareness to the degree that we believe in and practice separation.

> Take note of your intuitive promptings, and your confidence in things yet to be revealed.

Faith is the measure of our commitment to overcome separation, embrace the truth of our wholeness, and live without indulging illusions of failure, illness, or misery. Faith is the courage to be totally in present time, without any need for justification or reservation.

> Faith is a bond that holds firm our connection with all of life.

Faith is what was revealed to me by the miracle of *"The Lamb and The Lion."* It simply could not stay torn, because it lives in the fullness of each succeeding moment, in a perfect state of wholeness. When we have faith in our wholeness and the wholeness of all life, our vision is penetrating, our health radiant, our consciousness boundless, and our remembrance without flaw.

A frequent question students have asked me through the years is, "how could you possibly remember all the details of what Jesus said"? Well, I did take notes and kept a journal, but the greater reason is actually faith. In that moment I had the courage to listen with every particle of my being, nothing being hidden or held back. It was a moment of wholeness when 'all that I am' became the slate on which he wrote the message. Now all I have to do is shift into that state of wholeness, and all is remembered as if it were now, which it is. I don't live every moment of every day at that level of awareness. I have choices as everyone does, and sometimes the unknown and the uncertainty of new experiences can provide fuel for learning which is even more important. When we live in these occluded moments steeped in uncertainty, the key is to remember that even then we are whole.

"Now faith is the substance of things hoped for,
the evidence of things not seen." Heb. 11:1

Study Questions:

1. What is faith?
2. Where do your limitations come from?
3. What is restraining you from surrendering to that which you really want to have and receive?
4. How can fear of surrender, ironically, steer you directly into defeat, as well as impair your ability to win?
5. How is joy a completely different kind of happiness than anything our minds can imagine or conditions of life provide?
6. How does faith hold firm our connection with all of life?

Study Exercises:

1. Note a few times when you have "seen" beyond the ordinary.

2. Note a few times when you have solved a conflict by observing a difference in reality between participants in the conflict.

3. Note at least one time when faith became your guiding light.

4. Take note of your intuitive promptings, and your confidence in things yet to be revealed.

5. Note three instances in your life when surrender paid off in noticeable ways.

6. What are you resisting most now? What would it cost to surrender? What would be the results?

7. As you read about my challenge to surrender, consider your own invitations to surrender, and notice how you approach or resist these opportunities. Also, take note of what has happened in the past when you relaxed your resistance to change or accepted more of life.

My Personal Notes and Comments

Lesson 2

He Spoke

In Chapter 1 you were introduced to the multidimensional nature of our universe in which we can have many levels of experience depending on what our hearts seek, and where our faith and focus is leading. To go beyond our convenient patterns of reality, we are often required to pass through an initiation of surrender. But, what we are really surrendering is our own limited concept of "self" to a higher possibility, which is often the most arduous test of all.

Corresponding to the many dimensions of reality are also countless dimensions of our own consciousness which provide us with access, opportunity, and tools for seeking and processing experience. As I was to find out, these access points and faculties of consciousness are quite like the muscles of our body: they grow in strength and agility through use and exercise. First, we have to gain confidence that there is anything beyond our five physical senses and the ordinary reality created from their feedback.

Chapter 2 begins with the gentlest of exercises to that end. Jesus is calling my attention to diverse aspects of consciousness, first and foremost the difference between mind and heart. This chapter presents his first statement that the mind is a wonderful servant and a hard master. He lays the groundwork for later in-depth discussion of the heart as our higher intelligence.

Before I go into the particulars of that revelation, I want to first direct your attention to the way he "led" me by **getting my attention.** That would come first. Then he would direct my attention to one thing and another until I trusted the flow of expanding awareness. You may be saying to yourself, "how could he NOT have her attention, with such an amazing event happening in front of her?" But actually, the overwhelming nature of the moment and the wonderful specter of his Being caused me to act with great reserve, even perceptual deflection. Sometimes it was "too much." I was timid, averting my eyes, quiet as a mouse, and absorbed in my work until suddenly: HE SPOKE. It was only a short phrase, "Glenda, love is who you are." That is all he said for a while, but I was more "There."

Shortly after that he asked me about my strained eyes, which brought on the need for emotional openness, trust, and vulnerability. In retrospect that was a mild challenge, but it seemed like climbing a mountain at the time. Then with greater confidence I discussed a pet theory of mine, about which he was not terribly impressed. In that instance my ego was addressed and dismissed from the room. I had to decide, would "I" be fully present, or would I be there only as an insecure personality, executing my commissioned task?

Beyond my awareness he was subtlety calling forth and sculpting a greater presence for me while I was painting portrait of him! In looking back, it is clear that there were two portraitists in the room: one who paints on canvas and the other who creates through spirit. He did this by directing my attention to all the areas of consciousness that needed opening or cleansing and then filling them with fresh life. He brought my attention to life by being very attentive to me.

"He took pleasure in the things I enjoyed, was patient with my coffee breaks, amused himself with my procedures, and often made polite suggestions as to how I might do it better. He made me feel pretty, even though I usually wore blue jeans and sweatshirts; often had smears of oil paint on my face instead of makeup, and smelled of turpentine instead of roses. A perfect gentleman, he was kind, thoughtful and relaxed. Never in his presence did I feel inadequate. At the same time, He led me to heights of perception, understanding, and inspiration that would have been inconceivable only days before.

From the very beginning, I was amazed with how well he mastered the small as well as the large. The least thing, the simplest courtesy, the tiniest observation were all important to him."

The operative word here is **attentive!** Attention is the gateway to our consciousness and thereby to all forms of reality available to us. Jesus was always attentive, not only to me but to everything in the environment. And, he brought my attention to him through the little things that demonstrated love and caring. Unless he first accomplished that, I would not have heard much else he had to say.

> I cannot emphasize this enough: Through the mastery of little things we become strong. There are many BIG concepts in this book, but they will give you no advantage in life if you allow them to distract you from the very real small points to which you must give your attention daily.

"Beliefs and attitudes are the connecting links between the heart and mind. If you would see your hopes fulfilled, you must be very **attentive** to the foundations on which they are laid"

I have received thousands of letters through the years about how this book has changed some reader's life. In most of the letters there is a comment that reads a bit like this: "I have read many books of truth, but never have I read one before that revealed such profound truth in such a warm and caring human context, that made it all so real. Every time I pick up the book I discover something new, because it's really alive."

The reason for this is because the foundation of the book is based on complete attentiveness to being conscious in all the small yet pivotal gestures of communication as well as the major concepts. To Jesus, there is no order of importance with regard to consciousness. Consciousness is consciousness.

"Are not five sparrows sold for two pennies? And not one of them is forgotten before God. Why, even the hairs of your head are all numbered." Lu 12:6-7

So often we speak of "Christ Consciousness" and seek to emulate it, but rarely do we see the sweetness and simplicity of it. This is not to be missed if we would be like him.

Chapter 2 reveals the foundations of his whole message expressed through attentiveness and the growth of our relationship. Even though the text presents many interesting facets of reality and revelation, each of which could be a discussion in itself, the most important thing for you to observe at this point is the subtle process of creating and expanding consciousness through relationships with one another and with life. This process evolves as we surrender to our simple self, **being an observer** directing attention to an ever increasing circle of awareness, which we then **include as an extension of ourselves.**

This is what perception through the heart accomplishes. The opposite is prejudice and judgment, **which excludes and separates** everything from us that we cannot control. Initially our acts of judgment may be intended as discernment to support self-determination. Separation seems to increase one's control by providing more objectivity, but in the long run separation and judgment only consume the "consciousness muscle" pushing away that which we cannot control when true command of life is better served through the power of love. Judgment-oriented perception can generate prejudice and erosion of integrity. This is very subtle and deceptive in its early stages, often not revealing its bitter consequences until circumstances are painfully difficult to reverse.

24

This is the illustration that Jesus made in reference to the life of Judas. Judas was a devoted friend of Jesus and totally dedicated to the cause of liberation. He believed in goodness, but his ideas were entirely oriented toward confrontation and overthrow of government. This man, who valued goodness, blinded himself to the higher all-inclusive light of Christ through prejudice, separation, and judgment.

The tragedy of Judas was not limited to his betrayal of Jesus, but to himself as well! In so doing (and by extension) he betrayed the Christ Light offered to us all. His inner sense of guilt and hopelessness was so great that he completed the symbolism by taking his own life. His alienation is redeemable and his forgiveness assured whenever he realizes what he has done, who he **really betrayed**, and how it happened. Judas represents everyone operating under the delusion of separation; and the tragedy that comes from it. His place in the circle of twelve Apostles also symbolizes that all of humanity is invited to take Supper with the Christ, even in a state of error. It is WE who banish ourselves through our misuse of the invitation and failure to honor the truth of who we really are.

Chapter 2 contains many "appetizers" for the later banquets of revelation. He stunned me with new information every day; but, for the purpose of expanding consciousness, which was his primary motive. He also sparked a passion for exploring a new-found territory of awareness! What he did with me, he is also doing with you through **the way** everything is revealed. Please don't be dazzled with the ornaments (information), all the while missing the Christmas tree (foundation). Many of the "ornaments" were presented to me at this point just to "get my attention." Two thousand years ago he performed miracles for exactly that same reason.

Also, I ask that you don't allow the phenomenon of my extraordinary encounter with him to overshadow the growth of your personal relationship with him as you read these messages. My experience is now YOUR INSTRUMENT.

As you read this chapter, observe the way he introduced many of the most enlightened concepts first into the human context of ordinary experience. This is how and why he used parables long ago. Relate everything he says to YOUR personal experiences, and make them real for you.

I pray that you be patient to yourself and others, allowing inner growth to happen. One of my favorite teachings in Love Without End, which serves me every day, is about the 1% principle: *"The heart always brings new life to any situation and opens up possibilities that would have been impossible without it. Sometimes a 1 per cent change is enough to make all the difference, because that's all it takes to reposition a situation that seems to be absolute and to demonstrate that it is actually relative."*

This is regarding my "victory" on the subway, which you will find recounted in detail toward the end of chapter 2. Each positive decision I made that day caused a difference, which ultimately spared me (and others) from a disastrous encounter.

Pay attention to the small things in life which actually make a huge difference. Make notes of several goals, dreams, or tasks in life that you could make progress toward by using the 1% principle.

Be very observant of where your attention is drawn. This is how life calls you. You may follow your habitual inclinations or REDIRECT them to give more loving attention into areas that have been neglected or overlooked. If you have paid attention, a choice will be given to you. Remember, many of the choices that affect our lives are the small ones:

Study Questions:

1. What is the 1% principle?

2. How can we progress in our expansion of consciousness by paying attention to small things?

3. What was the real tragedy of Judas?

4. How do prejudice and judgment serve to separate us from what we cannot control? Examine the mechanism at work in your life.

Study Exercises:

1. Through the mastery of little things we become strong. Pay attention to the small things in life which actually make a huge difference. Make notes of several goals, dreams, or tasks in life that you could make progress toward by using the 1% principle.

2. Observe the way Jesus introduced many of the most enlightened concepts first into the human context of ordinary experience. This is how and why he used parables long ago. Relate everything he says to YOUR personal experiences, and make them real for you.

My Personal Notes and Comments

Lesson 3

The Wondrous Universe

This chapter presents his first detailed presentation of the basic building blocks of the universe. These apply to any universe, including your personal one.

"He described the components of the universe as being basically three. The first is love, the second is spirit, and the third is a substance that is finer than anything yet identified by science!"

He asked me to draw a triangle. I would suggest you do the same thing.

"At the top of the triangle he placed Love. *'The Source of Love is the Father, the Creator Himself, who is to all of existence like the sun is to life on earth. Yet, the light of His Love is so brilliant, only its halo can be perceived. The Source of Pure Love is the ultimate source of all love. From that Love you are emanated, or created. Like a ray of light, you are an entity of His Love. Love is the name of God, and Love is your name as well. In that, you are created in His likeness. You are known and shall always be known by the nature of your love.*

"Beyond the recognition of love, the presence and nature of God cannot be described, for Holy Presence is the definer, not the defined." No sooner had he said that than he anticipated my next question by adding, *"The Holy Trinity is also a sacred mystery which precedes and determines the tri-part universe. Like God, it cannot be defined, but is manifested*

29

everywhere in the very presence of all that exists. In the dimension of knowable reality, you might say that the one spirit is Holy whenever it manifests the presence of God, and the adamantine particles are literally the Body of God whenever they bring form to His will."

"Whenever he would direct his attention to the Father, his eyes would well. Perhaps it was partly because he was looking into a blinding light. However, the love and reverence he felt for his Father was more than even he could express in words. The emotions that poured from him were message enough."

It was clear that he was in love with God...not just in the sense of awesome grandeur, the Holy of Holies, or the presence of God he felt in himself, but also in every little creation or manifestation of life, including the presence of God he saw in me. Have you ever seen an old man look as his aging beloved wife and know that he only sees the beautiful sweetheart he fell in love with? He sees no lines, wrinkles, or gray hair, only the sparkling beauty of his true love and life mate. That's the kind of look I saw in Jesus. He was totally moved by the perfection his love beheld.

"The name of your Father is Love. And so, too, is that your immortal name. Love is the essence of true beingness. Love is not something that you do or don't do, give or don't give, receive or don't receive. In other words it is not a commodity, not a derivative substance. Love is not something that is subject to the laws of abundance or scarcity. Love is WHO you are."

"For that reason, love is ultimately unconditional. I am glad to hear people talking more about unconditional love today, but they would be more successful in their attainment of it if they knew why love is that way. Love is unconditional because it is your Origin, and who you are...not something that is done unconditionally."

Often our actions fall short, perhaps they are blocked by limiting circumstances, or other reservations we fear will be misunderstood or even abused. There is, however, nothing that can limit the love we ARE except our own decision to be temporarily "something else." The love that we are does not ask permission, and does not seek consent. It simply IS, by divine ordinance. Unconditional being is our ultimate state of love, and the secret to free will. Just be who you really are for long enough and that which you most desire will manifest.

"Actions are always conditional to some degree, because existence has conditions, and therefore, so do relationships. If love was only an action, there would be no escaping that fact."

We can only know the Presence of God by activating the power of love in ourselves and seeing it in others. Doing this completely and with mastery IS the Christ Presence.

"There was a sense of relief, as I settled down in my chair. I wanted to understand and practice unconditional love, but I had not wanted to be an unconditional doormat.

"The true nature of love is the answer to the riddle. The greatest mystery of the universe is that love is the sacred aspect of being. **Be it** to the fullest, and the rest of your life will fall into place.

"**The second great element of existence is spirit.** All things are of spirit." Pointing to the right corner of the triangle, He instructed me to write 'spirit'. "There is but one spirit. Spirit is in all things, around all things, with all things, and of all things. There is no such thing as spirit being isolated to a pure zone, apart from manifest creation." He cautioned that there have been many theories of matter versus spirit. "Such theories reflect an absence of real understanding and an obsession with the dualities of structured thinking. Inseparable and indivisible spirit is in all things. There is no place where spirit is absent. Spirit is one.

"Spirit must be understood as whole, continuous, and unbroken."

Spirit is the medium of all creation. Spirit recognizes each of our thoughts, ideas, and hopes, and receives them into its rich soil like a seed. When we honor the spirit through practicing wholeness, water the seed with love, and till the soil with your dedicated actions, the spirit will ALWAYS supplies our needs. If this seems to fail or is slow in coming, we need to ask ourselves: "Where did I break with wholeness, hold back my love, or become faithless in my lack of action?" Faith is a union and a partnership in which there is seamless dedication. Spirit is HERE, NOW with you.

"Whenever a person views spirit as the opposite of matter he has entered the world of misconception and duality. It is not true that Earth is material and Heaven is of the spirit. Spirit is the unity of us all, and of Heaven and Earth. It is through the oneness of spirit that the miracle of prayer can work. It is through the oneness of spirit that the power of dreams, of visions, and of prophecies can work. In the spirit we are one. Therefore in spirit we live one life, unified in a state of brotherhood, in a state of common awareness and seeking--either enlightenment and uplifting, or darkness and down pulling--whichever way one chooses it to be. Regardless of how your experience unfolds, we are of one spirit, and your experience is shared by all."

> There is one particle which creates its own energy. *'It's particle units are utterly generic in nature, and are the basic, irreducible components of physical existence.'* He called them "adamantine particles."

This particle is tinier than the atom or any of its component parts. As the ultimate simple particle, it is the irreducible building block of the universe. Comprehending this particle is currently a major objective in physics research. It is variously referred to by several names, including the Higgs boson, and some have even called it the "God Particle." There is, however, an ironic truth in that sarcasm. This particle is prior to the existing family tree of particles, which accounts for its difficulty in being studied. Apparently it creates mass, whereas other particles are the result of mass. This information is not to be underestimated in its importance. This is the particle that is expanding the universe. Only these prime particles can create a new supply of energy without "asking permission" from pre-existing forms and structures. Because it does not depend on preexisting forms of energy or structures, this primal energy can manifest miraculous healings or fulfillment of dreams. This is how Jesus multiplied the fishes. Once a particle has been committed to the matrix of structural organization, it can only acquire energy through exchange (law of conservation).

Now, let's see how he puts these three elements together:

> *"We are each known by our love. Spirit resonates to our love. It's just like a lake with many fish, where every fish sets off a different vibration within the water. So, too, your love resonates differently with the spirit than anyone else; like a fingerprint. And you may say this is what another's spirit feels like. But actually, this is how the spirit, the one and only spirit resonates to him. If you want the one and only spirit to resonate with you more affirmatively and distinctly, then truly be the love that you are."*

> *"The world would have you think that love is the consummating emotion of desired and pleasurable effects. In other words, that love is a created effect. Nothing could be further from the truth, for love is the universal instrument of initiating creation and then commanding it."*

In my many years of teaching and counseling, I have found that the main reason we do not see love as a causative force is that we are so addicted to giving and receiving it as a pleasure-based experience, like brownies with chocolate sauce and ice cream that makes us feel comforted or worthy. When we discover that it is even more delicious to cause and command love—because we ARE worthy to do so—we will have a new world!

> *"Love is the Source of everything. It is the commander and that command has been delegated to you as a child of love. This is why, in any situation, you can win by the power of love. Not by DOING LOVE. This is where you stumble. You have to BE LOVE! Love that is a burning fire at the heart of any situation. You can truly quell the storm by loving the forces that comprise it."*

That statement caused me to ask about his admonition to love our enemies. "I thought you would have realized by now that love has no opposites! Love is the solvent which ends all polarity."

33

> The perspective of love causes us to redefine who or what is our enemy.

The first thing to do in a high challenge situation is to flush out as many illusions as possible. Anything other than love has a large component of illusion. Sometimes our own projections or misperceptions create a false reality. Sometimes projections or misperceptions of another create illusions for them. Jesus never said we have to like cruel people or approve of destructive actions. What he meant is that the power of love RULES—everywhere in everything! When we come to a negotiating table with any goal in mind other than love, or some resolution leading toward love, nothing will be gained and conflict will resume. Nothing clears the air like an attitude of love toward what can be accomplished. After enough illusions have cleared from a situation, then you will be able to examine it more clearly and introduce love as a commanding and re-arranging force to permanently remove the danger. This process works with any kind of situation.

"If you want to remove pests from your house, love them into another place. There is no need to use chemical treatments when you understand the life follows love as a moth seeks the light. There are countless improvements you can make in your everyday life, simply by using love to command the adamantine particles."

At the same time we are cautioned to restrain ourselves from common misinterpretations of love, which counterfeit the power on lower levels of material accumulation and sensory indulgence. True love can release as easily as it can attach. It creates its own delight free from pleasure-seeking demands. There is a weed that can sometimes be mistaken for the flower of love, but it is filled with poison that discontents the soul. Its name is greed.

"GREED is the root of all evil. In the presence of greed, people go to extremes, and in the presence of extremes, the idea of scarcity is invented. When scarcity is invented, fear sprouts up like weeds in a garden. Every negative emotion known to man is born from fear.

34

"So that is the notorious family tree, from the roots to the branches. The extremes produced by greed beget scarcity, scarcity begets fear, and fear is the root of all destructive emotion and action."

"Fear abounds in the absence of love, and hatred is fear of love itself. Greed is an obsessive desire, which attempts to nourish and supply the needs of life without love. You might say greed is an attempt to counterfeit and to subvert the power of love. This is why it is the root of all evil. And it is not limited to material possessions or money. There can be greed for attention, influence, fame, education, therapy, dependency, even misery...anything which can establish bonds of attachment without love. So you are not wrong to consider that the absence of love brings problems. These are the greatest problems a person can have!"

"Why greed?"

"If you were trying to replace love utterly, how much would you need?"

"I get the point."

"Without love, a man has lost all bases for command. The best he can hope for is control, but that requires leverage...lots of it!"

"I suggested that you contemplate infinity and the abundance of the universe so that you can strengthen your connections to the rest of life, not that you would possess it all for yourself. There's a simple guideline which will give you unlimited potential for expansion without the perils of greed: Do not take more than you can truly love."

Second cousin to greed is the addiction many people have to use structure for their power and protection.

As Jesus explained, structure has intrinsic value to the organization of material existence, but it has very little value to the soul. "Don't try to own structure for its own sake. All structure is mortal. All structure fades away. I recommend that you store up your wealth in Heaven where the memory of your love will recreate all that is yours, leaving behind the structures which deceived you."

"Actually," He added, "This is the true blessing of the Sabbath. It is the day in which you release from your life any dominance of structure. You

35

behold the love of God, the infinity of the cosmos, the simplicity of spirit, and you rest. In so doing you are suspending artificialities and illusions which seek to possess you. In that state of relaxation you may return to the love that you are."

"Structure represents the predictable, agreed upon patterns of existence which start with simple forms and build up to complex ones. It is patterning that locks in the differences of potential, and holds organizational formulas in place. For example, structure is what makes the difference between steam, water, and ice even though the ingredients are the same. But structure is not the 'will' that determines whether H_2O will become steam or ice. That is determined by harmonic adaptations to the environment (love).

"All structure is derivative, and is subject to revision, suspension, or development. You might say that structure is the conservational imprint which allows desirable creations to be stabilized, retained, and combined into larger aggregates of form and matter. Structure is what holds things in place."

Our human attitudes toward structure are quite varied. There are those who have great respect for it, because they have gained power and profit in the world through structural organization, including social stratification. Others have similar disdain for structure as they do for greed, because they have been on the blunt end of its abuses. This is a subject worthy of us all to reexamine, regardless of our beliefs about it, because structure is an integral part of how the universe maintains itself, yet it is only an instrument of service and not worthy of the soul's homage. Abuse of structure has caused much pain, and greatly diminished the soul's mastery of life.

"Laid upon this grid work are many mind-generated patterns and structural models used by man for control. There are no 'sacred designs' preceding reality. This idea has been invented to make you afraid to revise or to dispense with unworkable structures, and to give structures dominance over you."

Occasionally, when I think about structure, I compare it to the 'save' button on a computer. It's a memory that lets us retain and integrate one formulation into another, or to bring up a program again in another time and place where it might be more useful. It's comforting to know that structure is only as important as it serves the ongoing creations of love. It's reassuring to also remember there's a 'delete' button which restores life back to original potential!

I asked him about life after death, and what it was like to experience the physical disintegration and spiritual continuity.

"Life as you know it here is too structured for you to perceive your greater continuity. All that is really you continues. Life just leaves its complex form. All of the adamantine particles that make up your body remain with you. You are remembered in the spirit forever, and the love that you are will always carry your sacred name. As you are remembered and cherished by spirit, your recreation occurs again and again throughout eternity, whether it be in heaven, on earth, or anywhere else in your Father's infinite domain."

Eventually, I had the courage to use the word "reincarnation." "What do you have to say about the subject of past and future lives?"

His reply was to the point, as usual. *"Your immortality is a simple thing, and so your understanding will be more accurate if you keep it simple as well. By the will of God, life creates a place for you infinitely again and again, according to your love and in relation to your loved ones."*

However, *"The philosophy of reincarnation is not that simple. It does affirm your continuity, and that is good. However, there's a twist in it that defers your immortality back to structure of time and generations of evolution, which is not true. Your immortality is not imprisoned within a wheel of life, or pathway of cause and effect. Neither are you the product of linear evolvement. You were created in perfection, and perfect love, and you do continue to re-manifest infinitely, but it is according to the will of the Father, and according to your own purposes, your own love, and your own place of service and learning."*

He added, with a touch of humor, *"You actually have only one life! It's just a very long one, with many chapters."*

I laughed, and all seriousness disappeared. Reincarnation is a choice, but not the only option. Immortality can be experienced many ways. Remember that free will is the first principle upon which our life was created. Our very nature is love, and from these gifts our lives take shape.

This chapter ends on a very powerful statement about our origins as a soul and the birth trauma that many still carry with them. Unfortunately, this original birth of self was experienced as separation and has been dramatized as such ever since. This had value in that it led us toward countless pathways of experience, all of which have developed and enhanced our individuality. Now is the time to rise above that trauma and to see our birth as the most wonderful gift of self and the eternal union with our creator and our fellow participants in creation. Please take this to heart in terms of your own feelings and issues.

"How much more significant it will be when the soul recognizes its duress and awakens to its magnificent endowment."

"What is preventing the realization?"

"People are torn between wanting to go Home and fearing the loss of personal identity and freedom...wanting to stay apart and fearing the perils of becoming lost. It must be realized that even though you are one with the Father, you will never be re-absorbed into collective anonymity. Having his own place within the one spirit honors each person, and there will never be a time after which you are not.

"You have been given eternal life in your own name. When you are able to comprehend the grandeur of that gift, you will be able to experience your birth anew with ecstasy.

"You viewed it as separation the first time and have dramatized and structured it as separation ever since."

The points in this chapter are so deeply significant to the rest of the book, it is important to pause, savor, and integrate your present understanding. These ideas will be presented again in other contexts and you will see them applied in different ways. What you understand NOW is enough for how you are NOW. Let's gather that in.

Study Questions:

1. What are the three component parts of the universe? What part is unconditional? What part is "one"? What part has endless energy?

2. What is structure? When is it beneficial? How can too much of it suppress love and impair free will?

3. What particle is the source for its own energy, and is therefore inextinguishable?

4. What is the one sure way we can know the presence of God?

5. How is greed the root of all evil?

Study exercises:

Create the following lists. They will give you important bench-marks to refer to in the future and as you see your consciousness growing.

1. List the five points of information that stood out the most when you read this chapter, points that you grasped with an "ah-ha."

2. List the five points of information that you want to return to at a later time after you have assimilated the current impact.

3. List the five ways your consciousness or life can or will be changed by what you have just realized.

My Personal Notes and Comments

Lesson 4

The Love That You Are

This lesson begins with the first words Jesus spoke to me. "Love is who you are."

Without first establishing love as a noun which we can use for God, our self, and others, there is nothing to join in love. When love is only seen as an action, feeling, or experience, it happens and passes on. Eternity rests in the noun. Much in the same way (though stated differently), God clarified to Moses, "I AM not just the one who "does and creates," I AM the one who IS.

In a universe driven by energy, in a world driven by action and competition, it's easy to miss the fact that the real power of love rests in its BEING. From that, all actions come.

The most perfect example of love applied to creation, from the center of Self is God the Father. Next after that would be Jesus life on earth and his eternal life. However, there are others among us that model this truth, and not all of them famous or brilliant people. Some of them may have been friends, family members, teachers, coaches, or exemplary people you have admired from history. Their greatest legacy to you is being this kind of model. Be grateful for how they raised our

41

expectations for our self, if only a bit, study their lives and learn what you can from their journey. I think there is no more beneficial literature than biographies of people who have some mastery or sterling break-through to discovery of the love that they are. Even fiction of such discovery cannot exist except that someone has witnessed this happening in real life.

Beyond this, when we speak of love, we are honoring the highest and dearest connections we have with one another. In regard to others, love is about union. We could like someone or something a lot, but until we feel union with it or them what we feel is not yet love. Love between and among us is known by the union we share. This could be on all levels of family relationships, with our closest friends, and even those with whom we share a common purpose at work or common values in life. Once more we are talking about 'being,' this time about shared being, one to another through some common bond.

By extension of unity, love makes all the difference with the goals, purposes, and activities of your life. Love determines your potential for success, and the dedication you are willing to make in pursuit of it.

The love we seek does not come from the outside world. It comes from the unions we create that cause the outside world to vanish.

His emphasis was on the nature of being love versus doing love. This is the whole key to unconditional love. Many people are seeking to practice unconditional love today...truly wanting to experience that way of being, but finding their way blocked by merciless obstacles. After all, who wants to be an unconditional doormat? Who wants to be unconditionally stupid? No sooner do we seem to have transcended a condition and loved beyond it than it snaps back in our faces! How do we love unconditionally and also take into account the fact that life has conditions to it? He helped me find the answer to that riddle.

His comments were, "*As long as you consider love to be an external force, it will always be subject to the conditions of life. Life does have its conditions. Nature has its conditions.*"

You've heard it said that life is about connecting the dots. That pertains to both the internal and external world, except that the dots outside our self are easier to see! To help clarify our inner vision let's imagine that every dot of inner discovery left a footprint in the sand. Now envision connecting those to see what portrait has been created.

Most often the designs of our life are not pre-created or even preconceived. Almost always they emerge from the process of living and discovery. All design, whether of life or art is about making connections, but most of all, it's about learning to BE the CONNECTOR.

"Life is an adventure in connecting. The connections you make affirm and strengthen your character.

"The soul is crying for a reality experience which only physical life can give to it. The body is crying for an immortality experience, which only the soul can give to it. As you permit this union to fulfill itself, you will directly know what it feels like to be the love that you are.

"Man was created through progressions of unity--first with God, then with life, and last but not least by marriage of body and soul. As a child of God, man was given a sense of self, with a secondary covenant to accept it. The body needs to acknowledge the soul in order to have a higher life. The soul needs to honor the body in order to fulfill its physical experience. The body and soul have much to offer each other."

...

"Your first duty is to accept the union of body, soul, and love that exists within and as yourself. How can a woman find her place in the world or a man make peace with his brother when neither has successfully made the most critical integration of their lives?

"Wholeness is Holy; wholeness is healing. That is the essence of all miracles--physical, mental, financial, and social. Whatever has been torn apart comes back together into a state of wholeness. Love supports wholeness, and wholeness supports love. Through that common bond, love can heal anything."

If you think about it, that's what Jesus did for the human race. He became us in order to demonstrate what words cannot convey. Even now he is willing to BE anyone who will invite him in. He does not want to replace anyone's own unique existence, but he sees us struggling to find our self and wants to help us find the center from which we can pull the points of our life together.

With the idea I'm presenting, there is a higher suggestion that we learn to share life with others who have come to offer us a hand. Through our joined hands we create a larger more sweeping picture than we could ever do alone. Love is the power that brings this about. Love is the power behind our creativity. But, more importantly, it's the only power that can conquer our ego. You see, the problem with surmounting our ego is that we actually need a center to our being! In the absence of LOVE as that center, we will fill it with something else, whatever works— some form of identity, role in a story, or characteristic ability. For me that would have been "artist" if I had not grown to a larger meaning of the ability and found a more expanded context in which to explore my value to others.

The problem with our early formed ego-centers is that they were chosen and established at a time when we needed to take our place in the world. Therefore, they became associated with survival, identity, and rights we command in life. To invalidate one's ego or to suppress it, just invites reaction and over compensation. To destroy one's ego with self-deprecation creates a false humility that parades as unworthiness. ONLY love, the love that you are, can overcome ego and transform it into a worthy and powerful center for your life.

Discovering the love that "you are" is often quite a process; yet, none more worthy of your life. To know this, and to attach your actions of love and your acquisitions of love to that is to be adding bricks to your mansion in the kingdom of heaven. Without that knowledge many of our actions of love are like sand-castles that wash away in the ebbing and flow of tides.

Jesus said, "Love can also mean letting go. The pain of this realization might be unbearable if it were not fully understood that the power of love lies in the depth of your being. Releasing attachments, as an act of love, is the most difficult expression for anyone. Second to that is

44

the releasing of hatred and fear through forgiveness. Forgiveness could take on a more positive meaning if it were observed as an act of perfecting the love that you are. Last, but not least, love may require that you release your compulsive urge to do something when there is nothing for you to do. Like the Holy Father, who rested in order to command by love, so too is that an option for you. There are times when doing nothing is the greater expression of love, and the ultimate expression of being. All leverage over you ceases when you understand these things."

What makes it so difficult to let go of goals that failed or relationships that didn't work is not the unproductive side of it all. That's easy. It's the love we had invested in it! It haunts us, it commands our unrelenting attachment, we continue to wonder what went wrong, and after all, we loved at some point. It's as if a piece of our self has broken off and is begging to be rescued. That analogy is not too far off point. What we are not "getting" is that this would not have happened if we had not invested love externally that was not acceptable to the love that we ARE. Either we would have been successful, or the love we invested would have been retrieved at an earlier point of responsibility. When we are fully in touch with our love, we are in a state of integrity that manages life more benevolently for all.

With even the best of intentions, when love is offered as an action it is often rejected or responded to with hostility. This is because it was received as a judgment or opinion from the other person's viewpoint.... rather than love. Jesus said when you are being the love that you are, you will be led to right action.

You were created in the image of God who is the Source of all love, but how can that be true, considering all the diversity of forms and imperfection in the human race?

"An instructive analogy which you might consider is the role of DNA in your own body as a language base for the body's integrated performance. You could take tissue samples from different parts of your body and DNA analysis would identify them all as being uniquely yours. However, not one of these tissue samples is equal to the whole body, nor

could any one of them function alone. Yet the fact of a common DNA code allows all facets of the body to cohere and to work together in a coordinated fashion. You might say that there is a common encoding of DNA 'as love' that you share with your Heavenly Creator, which allows you to act in coordinated service to the greater whole of life as well as to all the manifestations of it."

> There are two central themes in this chapter, which are ultimately just two aspects of the same thing: Love and Being.

All the other teachings, even structure, scarcity, and worldly experience, are simply topics that call forth the need for mastering the power of Love and Being. It is essential for you to know this in order for your studies not just to enrich your intellect, but also ignite the presence of Christ within. In the words of Jesus:

"From the beginning there have been three holy elements--the three pillars of Being. The first and the Ultimate is the I AM presence, which is the Source of Divinity. After that is Innocence, which is the spiritual presence of Divinity. And third, there is Love, which is the manifest presence of Divinity and its power of creation. All three aspects of being are extended to man for his blessing and fulfillment."

"Love is the imprint of your beingness."

"Love is a quality, unbounded by fences and magnitudes, which derives its power from God, the ultimate Source of Love. As such, love has some inalienable rights. First of all, you have the simple right to honor within yourself all that love has brought you, and to assimilate those things into your character. For your character is the summarization of your love. No one can ever take that from you."

"Love is universally free. Thus, in being love, so are you. Your body may be imprisoned, but your love has no boundaries.

"Love commands the adamantine particles, thus in being love you take command of your life.

"Love is the master of conditions, not the servant of them. Thus in being love, you are no man's slave.

"Love is the law, and any law is only as valid as it is rooted in love. By this, all men shall know the law, and be equal under it. This is why I left you

with only two commandments: To love God with all your heart, and your neighbor as yourself."

"Love is universally resonant with all of life, and in being love you are also resonant with life. There are no conditions to the truth of who you are. It is your sacred right to be the love that you are, and that is unconditional."

Often we think of love as only a passionate, grand, or intensely dedicated feeling. But, if love is who we are, then obviously it has to be present in the "trenches of life" and the ordinary feelings as well.

"In the trenches, love is knowing that your very presence makes a difference. It means being true to your own calling and capacity for service, refusing other calls to riches and fame, which could diminish the glory of your real character. It often means standing firm in the midst of chaos, with patient conviction that you hold a piece of the unfolding puzzle. Love is a businessman who persists with dedication and clarity through many sleepless nights of high demands upon low budgets until a solution appears. Love is a devoted and patient mother who never ceases in her vigilance to heal and redirect her restless, troubled child."

So often, however, when we find ourselves in the trenches of life we seek refuge in our castle, draw the bridge and fill the mote with water. In other words, we look for cover and protection behind structure. **The irony Is that structure is one of the great contributing factors of human suffering.** It is ridged and we are fluid. It is dead and we are alive. Excessive dominance of structure causes pain and does not contribute to our healing, other than providing hospital beds and a medical system that could be improved with more love and less structure.

"When structure is out of balance or in conflict with itself you are going to feel pain." He added, *"Even greater pain comes when structure is in conflict with love, and you do not know how to resolve the conflict. The answer lies in knowing the correct priority and in understanding the*

greater dimensions of the heart to master any situation. Structure is no match for the heart except to make the heart strong."

Love and structure are not opposites. They are just alternative modes for managing life. Even if you chose structure, love would still be there. Even if you chose love, structure would still be there...but in a different level of importance and influence. What makes you a Child of God instead of just a creation of God is that you have the power to consciously CHOOSE love.

I am trusting that you will not use Jesus' teaching as an invitation to rebel against structure, for you would not like an environment without it (chaos) any more than you like environments where structure in a dominant priority.

You simply must answer one question, because you cannot serve two masters. Which will hold to the highest priority in your life, love or structure?

This is followed by one of the most important passages in LWE, which is the key to attaining Christ consciousness and a life that can be lived in full connection with the world and yet remain unattached to the worldly pressures.

"Love opposes nothing, but conquers all. Love is in the world but not of it! Fear and hatred, and the evils that come from them, are all derivative. Love is primary. Love existed before the universe, and most certainly before the structures of the world. In the beginning there was no evil, fear, or hatred. There was only One Love, One Body of Potential, and One Spirit. As manifestations began to take shape, free will was extended to every aspect of love, to be life, to experience life, to fulfill its potential, and to know itself as love. There was even the choice to deny its own nature, if that should be desired. From this last choice all the 'weeds' of peril have sprung.

"This last choice was a very important gift. For without it you would have been an aspect of love without the power to forward creation. You would have been a creation of God, but not a Child of God. Once love has

48

become your choice as well as your nature, all potential for duality is erased from your life, and you are given command."

Here are some daily practices that will help you build or repair connections in your life. You can make it into a Spiritual Spa to refresh your sense of Love and Being:

1. Begin (or end) your day with some expression of gratitude and appreciation.
2. Next, forgive something. There is always something or someone to forgive, because forgiveness is just letting go of some disappointing attachment. Attachment reduction is wonderful way to lighten your load.
3. Practice innocent perception. Just be with a perception, experience or observation without feeling that you need to embellish or develop it into more than it is. Just let a tree be a tree, a squirrel be a squirrel and then follow the thread into a widened circle of innocent perception.
4. Watch the sunrise or sunset.

Study Questions:

1. When does liking become love?
2. What is one of the major contributors of human suffering?
3. Why should we manage structure with love instead of rebelling against it?
4. What is the best way to hold unconditional love?
5. How can doing love before first being it get us in trouble?
6. What is the only power that can conquer your ego?
7. Why is it sometimes so difficult to let go of losing situations or failures?

Study exercises:

1. Locate five instances when you were able to **be** love without **doing anything;** times when you just held firm to your true nature regardless of what was going on around you.

2. Show how connections lead to union and union to love, whether within yourself, of between yourself and others.

3. List some of your own examples about love in the ordinary situations of life.

4. When has structure "gone too far"? Make up your own examples.

5. Find five areas in your life where there is either too much structure or too little structure and write a brief plan about how to bring structure back to moderation and service to life and love.

6. Study how our mastery of structure can improve even the smallest of events. Take a club meeting for instance. If no duties or leadership were assigned, everyone talked at once, and no regular meeting times or places were set, no one knew if there would be a speaker, projects, or refreshments this would be a pretty pathetic non-entity. It would soon dissipate. On the other hand, if the same rules of order have prevailed for five generations, only a small power clique controlled, nothing new ever happened, everyone paid dues but they only served "status quo." If every meeting was in the same place with the same speaker and same stale cupcakes and English tea what value does it have for life? Structure is at its best when it is in a dynamic interchange with love and life and serves them both. The answer is to BE love and master structure.

My Personal Notes and Comments

Lesson 5

The Adamantine Particles

It hardly matters where we begin with the subject of adamantine particles, as long as we understand that all manifestation ultimately traces back to, and embodies, their nature and potential. The knowledge of adamantine particles is not limited to particle physics, galactic travel, or ethereal realms. It is critical to our understanding of life as we live it. It has been said that the air we breathe has also been breathed by all living entities. That thought was expanded for me through my new understanding of the adamantine particles and their river of living supply.

"They are the fundamental building blocks of physical existence—particularized energy potentials which activate, unify, and give form to infinity. As points, they are irreducible, indivisible, and generic; and their very existence establishes dimension. Between one point and another, there is dimension. Between a series of points, there is a pattern of dimension. Thus there is space. The dynamic of energy exists through rhythmic activation and repetition of these patterns. Matter is formulated as these patterns and rhythms become more complex and specialized."

"Adamantine particles are the only particles that **actually create mass**. Simply put, they are the primary emanation points where energy and mass are the same. The matrix from which they spring is the *continuous filament of undefined potential, which is the eminent and undivided presence of the one spirit.*

Even though I was unfamiliar with the word "adamantine" when Jesus first introduced it to me in 1992, it has been around for thousands of years. In English, the word adamantine means "something extremely hard or unyielding," in fact, "adamant." It is also an adjective to qualify something as "hard and brilliant as a diamond." In the Buddhist tradition, we can find one of the first references to this word; in Sanskrit Vajra means adamantine, and Vajradhatu is a Sanskrit word which means "adamantine sphere." Perhaps the most important finding, however, was that the word Vajrasattva means "the Adamantine Being" who represents the Buddha of purification and healing. The Vajrasattva meditation is a special practice recommended by Vajrayana Buddhism to their practitioners who wish to cleanse themselves from impurities accumulated and caused by negative feelings, thoughts, words, and actions. Clearly, in these ancient usages there is a direct correlation between this particle and the soul which engages with it.

The term 'particle' is used here in the context of subatomic particles. We can say that "adamantine particles" mean "pure particles," not combined with anything. They are particles so pure, small, and simple they cannot be divided and therefore, are fundamental particles. The adamantine particles form all elements of the Universe. They are the smallest, indivisible particles that comprise the atoms of all original substances like oxygen, nitrogen, iron; in other words, everything that is, including our bodies

In the chain of creation, the adamantine particles precede all other manifestations, including light. Not only scientifically, but also scripturally we are told that 'something' preceded light. That 'something' does not behave with any of the linear predictability of light or any other particle, which would be constant to the speed of light or resulting from it. That 'something' is observable only through motion, compression, expansion, and spontaneous emission of mass generating energy (adamantine particles). That 'something' is the 96% dark energy and dark matter existing outside the atomic field. It is called 'dark' because it preceded (and exists beyond) the field of light; however, it is anything but negative. It is intensely "alive," moving, and responsible for the infinite expansion of our universe. It is 'dark' only to our current instruments, but it is replete with motion, is spontaneous, will compress to emit particles with mass, and will then deliver enough energy for these particles to aggregate with other particles to create atomic structures, and there is massive scientific evidence for its existence. According to Jesus, this is a pre-creation dimension of pure potential that responds to love, thought, and feeling.

There is an intriguing scientific book titled "Something Called Nothing," or to put it more correctly, from empty space, the vacuum, the void. Scientifically, this is referred to as a zero-point field. It gives rise to continual fluctuations and potential for spontaneous integration and disintegration. Knowledge of this opens up a whole new world for us to explore. Like the strings of an unseen puppeteer, this field holds all matter under its influence. It's like water to a fish, an essential ingredient of the universe. Once physicists understand this pervasive, unseen influence, they will be able to answer a question so fundamental that ancient thinkers probably never even dared to ask it: "Why does matter have mass?"

Jesus has told us that an adamantine particle is the mass resulting from spontaneous integration within the zero-point field. Then, all other particles derive their mass from the actions and accumulations of these fundamental particles. Until the zero-point field is explored and better understood, these particles will not be discovered.

So, let's review for a moment the current state of quantum mechanics and its explanation of the universe. There is really no way to reduce this subject to simple clarity without a small science lesson. If you are not familiar with, or comfortable with science, better to hear this synopsis from me, because I will use common English as much as possible and have empathy for any struggle you may feel for this daunting subject.

Also, I feel it's very important that you learn about adamantine particles in a reliable context of scientific reality lest you come to believe that we are referring to some kind of mystical essence that has no place in the landscape of scientific phenomena. As a matter of fact, quantum physicists are making research of this particle one of their highest priorities at this very turn in the road of human history. They believe all of our new energy systems depend on its discovery, not to mention our expanded and enhanced understanding of the universe and its origins.

Matter is composed, on a tiny scale, of particles called atoms. Atoms are in turn made up of a very small nucleus surrounded by a cloud of particles called electrons. Scientists of the early 20th century found they could not explain the behavior of atoms using only the structural models provided by traditional physics. Therefore, they developed a new interpretation of matter and energy to describe atoms. They formulated the quantum theory, or quantum mechanics. Quantum theory describes matter as acting both as a particle and as a wave. In the visible objects encountered in everyday life, the wavelike nature of matter is too small to be apparent. Wavelike nature becomes important, however, in microscopic particles such as electrons, which behave like waves. They exist as a fuzzy cloud of negative charge around the nucleus of an atom, instead of as a particle located at a specific point.

Quantum mechanics revealed deeper layers of energy composition inside ordinary matter. The nucleus of an atom, for example, is made of particles called protons and neutrons, which are themselves made up of even smaller particles called quarks. There are other particles that cannot be broken down any further, and these are called fundamental particles. These fundamental particles provide the basic units that make up all matter and energy in the Universe. A fundamental particle is infinitely small; it exists at a certain point in space without taking up any space. These fundamental particles are, therefore, impossible to see directly, even with the most powerful microscopes. Instead, scientists must deduce the properties of such a particle from the way it affects other objects.

At the 'known' edge of the atomic universe, fundamental particles have already been found that cannot be divided into smaller particles. However, they are not the adamantine particles spoken of by Jesus, because they are the products of **prior division**, as demonstrated by the fact that they each have an anti-particle equivalent. Obviously, something preceded them. Even so, they are interesting particles which form the foundation of manifest reality. As a class they are referred to as Leptons, which includes electrons, muons, and neutrinos.

Neutrinos are fundamental particles with no electric charge and almost no mass; they cannot be broken into smaller particles. Neutrinos are so small they pass right through most material, and are probably the first particles to immerge into the dimension of light and structure, forming 'this side' of the division between created and pre-created matter. Neutrinos are the transitional particles between Dark Matter and Light Matter.

Neutrinos and Electrons are the 'bridge' particles, existing on the threshold between the zero-point field and the atomic field. It has been seen that electrons continually radiate away their energy as predicted by classical theory, but simultaneously absorb a compensating amount of energy from the ever-present sea of zero-point energy in which the atom is immersed. An equilibrium between these two processes leads to the correct values for the parameters known to define the ground-state orbit.

Because of this ceaseless activity, atomic collapse is prevented, entropy does not consume the universe, and expansion continues forever. The very stability of matter itself appears to depend on the presence of the underlying sea of zero-point energy.

On the 'source' side of this bridge we have the zero-point field which provides an inexhaustible supply of motion in a state of dynamic equilibrium. This field also spontaneously generates an endless supply of adamantine particles. Correlated, these two functions provide the origin of both motion and mass, the primal ingredients of energy. Zero-point fields drive particle motion, and the sum of particle motions throughout the universe in turn generates the zero-point fields. This is a kind of self-regenerating cosmological feedback cycle quite like a cat chasing its own tail.

In this pre-creation field of pure motion and spontaneity there is no resistance. Therefore, any form of energy generated by friction would simply dissipate. There would be nothing to resist it. Force does not work here. Nevertheless, adamantine particles (the substance generated by this zone)

> *Essentially, this field is intelligent and responds to subjective influence ranging from primal instinct, to feeling, thought, and most of all Love. It is also highly 'magnetic' in the sense of drawing to itself that which will contribute to more creation.*

need "power" to build the other particles and atoms. How is this accomplished with only one type of energy being compatible with them? The native energy matrix of adamantine particles is simply endless motion. But, upon closer observation we see that this motion can expand, compress, or form directional patterns. This is the point where Consciousness (or Higher Mind, if you will) connects to the realm of manifestation through projections of intention affecting feeling. This is the connective tissue of our Universe, having for its outflow the Universal Life Force. Love is not only the most beautiful of feelings, it also is the power that ignites and directs adamantine particles into manifestation. This is accomplished through the dynamic connection of feeling and intention.

What this means to you as students of life, spirituality, wholeness, and healing is that there is a pre-manifestation energy that will respond to your love, thoughts, feelings, prayers, and desires. This energy potential is the source of adamantine particles, which are already infinite and growing in the universe. This fountain of life is your assurance of your continuance in this universe not only as a spiritual being, but also as a creative manifesting soul capable of fulfilling your place in existence. There is no inevitable or eventual scarcity, and there is plenty of energy and substance for every good idea.

Love is the ultimate force in the Universe; it holds every galaxy, star and planet in its place. In the presence of love, patterns of beauty, perfection, harmony, and efficiency manifest spontaneously.

He assured me of a profound change that will occur when the foundation of our understanding shifts from force to attraction. *"Magnetic attraction explains the greater unity of existence, and it is actually magnetic cohesion that integrates inter-dimensional fields, which in turn support and connect all physical reality. Infinity is **not** the left over. Infinity is the unifying factor that **integrates everything**. When man's basis of thinking changes from force to attraction, every aspect of technology will change as well."*

With regard to human potential, the heart is your magnetic center. It is through your heart that you are attracting adamantine particles and by your love that you command them." He said that adamantine particles respond to magnetism under the influence of love.

"Only the true heart can sense the vital flow and exchange of particle energy. This is why you are more intuitive in the areas of your greater devotion. When the Sacred Heart comes to life again and its fire glows within, you will begin to magnetize a fresh supply of adamantine particles from an infinitely abundant universe. There is no limit to the adamantine particles that can be drawn to you. These can be used for empowering your life, healing it, and lifting it to a much higher state of performance."

Study Questions:

1. What commands the adamantine particles?
2. What is Jesus' definition of life?
3. What is your magnetic center that attracts adamantine particles and then carries them into manifestation?
4. Can adamantine particles be seen directly? What are some examples of that?

5. Jesus talks about the true law of ownership. How does this relate to the adamantine particles? What is really yours?
6. What does he mean by adamantine memory?
7. Jesus talks about three levels of understanding in the universe. The first is survival, and the second is cause and effect. What is the third level, and how is that level of understanding necessary to begin commanding the adamantine particles?
8. How does Jesus explain karma, and what is above karma?
9. Consider all the substance and energy of life that you have inherited from others and those who came before. How can you be a better steward of that inheritance and also create your own legacy?
10. What would be a good (and workable) correlation of food and love **for you?**

Manifesting your heart's desire:

There is a wonderful manifesting process that utilizes the hearts magnetic power to attract adamantine particles (and Love's command over them) and direct them toward fulfillment. This can help you with any desire that you truly conceive and hold in your heart. Here are the steps:

1. Discover, choose, or reveal a desire that your heart can support. The main discernment here is to see the difference between needs, wants, and compulsions driven by other forces.
2. Hold it close to your heart. Cup your hands about a foot out from your heart and visualize holding your desire as if it were a baby bird. Now, start drawing it close to your heart in full certainty that it has already been born and is growing in the universe even now.

3. Clear it. An interesting thing happens as you begin to gently (and physically) move your chosen desire closer to your heart.

Every objection of your mind and every emotional denial will raise its "voice" and let you know why you cannot get or achieve what you truly want. If you hold the vision firmly and move it toward your heart without reservation, you will get to see every difficulty that will be cast in its path. Many of these "objections" will be implanted doubts, some will be insecurity about what others will say, and most will just be the ranting of an unruly mind. As each objection causes a halt to your movement, just acknowledge it and decide what the appropriate handling is without allowing it to stop you. Repeat this process until your hands can deliver the new-born desire into your hearts safe keeping and your hands are firmly crossed over your heart.

4. Live it. Remember that life is love in action. As you live your desire, you allow love to command in a more dynamic way. An example could be as simple as this. If your desire is to visit your family in Europe, it could begin with a telephone call to the relatives. That's a kind of visit in itself, but in it you will all solidify your plans and form a realistic budget. You may not yet be able to afford the ticket, but a call to a travel agent can set the alert for specials and bargains. Making sure that you have adequate vacation time from work can remove obstacles, not to mention updating your passport. Then every day when you arise, just imagine waking up in your chosen destination and preparing for breakfast with your family. If you have the visionary strength and emotional courage to act as if it has all been ALREADY given, there is no way that you will not fulfill your dream! This is the very anatomy of FAITH, which we will study more extensively in another context.

5. Relax so that the universe may fulfill it in holistic time (not necessarily linear cause and effect.) and give rise to spontaneous opportunities for attaining your desire.

My Personal Notes and Comments

Chapter 6

The One Spirit

Jesus referred to spirit as one of three great pillars of existence. Love, adamantine particles, and spirit are landmarks of our consciousness, not because they are each separate entities, but rather because each denotes a principle aspect of existence, which lends intelligence and connection and understanding to the acts of creation.

The One Spirit is endless and awesome, impossible to define conclusively. Moreover, if we consider that One Spirit connects all things, sustains all things, and is the indivisible oneness of all existence, then from what vantage point could we objectively describe it? Since the very nature of definition is to objectify, contain, and establish that which is and is not, how could we even conceive an absolute definition of our oneness? So, let us marvel at the simplicity of infinite inclusion. In referring to spirit, we are reverently acknowledging and invoking the presence of that which unifies and connects all of existence. There is no place where spirit is not. That is the beauty and the glory of our oneness.

Everything that you see and touch is spiritual essence slowed down so that it appears to be coalesced mass. There are six primary densities of

The Spirit world
The thought world
The feeling world
The sound world
The light world
The material world

63

spiritual essence in approximately this descending order:

Each of these can be measured by instruments, elevated by love, corrupted by negativity, disentangled by meditation, and healed by prayer.

You cannot know the meaning of your life until you are connected to the power that created you. You are not your body; you are not your mind; you are Love existing in spirit…this is the greatest truth. This is the truth that will set you free.

As you study this chapter, absorb it intuitively and with compassion, realizing that everything in your life is spirit in one form or another. This is why it is so hard to "see spirit." You are totally immersed in it! However, spirit does reveal itself. From your personal perspective there are basically five ways in which you will see spirit revealing itself to you. Notice how this happens in real life for you and others.

1. As the one unified and indivisible matrix of all existence. This is where we are finding new enlightenment with science and spirituality merging into harmonious and shared realizations.

2. As that which defines and supports your own intangible and immortal nature, and provides you with the etheric substance for thought, feeling, imagination, and intuition.

3. As that which provides your intangible attraction for and connection with others.

4. As that which provides constant guidance for you and preserves your original state of oneness with God while you explore the worldly realms of discovery and adventure. This we call the Holy Spirit.

5. As that which lifts you up to a higher plane above the worldly problems and duress.

Study Questions:

All of these questions are answered in this chapter. Sometimes it's more enlightening to start with the right question and let the answer find you in the midst of your search.

1. What are the three most prevalent misconceptions about spirit in the world today?

2. How does your experience "as spirit" give you a different viewpoint than your experience 'as love'? Both of these perceptions are native to you and simply different sides of your own immortal presence.

3. What is the major defining difference between spirit and the adamantine particles?

4. As mankind awakens to the unbroken essence of spirit, what kind of gifts and abilities will also be born?

5. What is the "bridge to communication" to which Jesus refers?

6. What is the limitation of all force-based thinking, action, and engineering?

7. Are there others like us elsewhere in the universe?

8. What does Jesus mean by, "Evil is derivative, not primal?"

9. What is Heaven? What is Hell?

10. Recall some real time examples of the "hundredth-monkey" phenomenon. This could be as simple as when you and your family all had the same idea at the same time, or as large as when you thought of something that was already becoming a major trend but you did not yet know it.

Exercise: "See It Done for Another"

Because of the inclusive and reciprocal nature of spirit, we can see it more clearly through our relationships to others. We have all heard the Golden Rule, "To do unto others as you would have them do unto you." This, of course, draws its truth and power from the fact that within our One Spirit, everything that goes around, comes around. This is timeless, good advice. However, such ideas are usually presented as reminders to act with consideration and restraint regarding the rights and well-being of others rather than giving us ideas of how to creatively assert ourselves **with the good of others in mind**. We will now take that same truth and shape it into an active creative process for achieving our goals in life.

Because it is unified and indivisible, the power of spirit is intensified when it is shared with others. Another interesting observation about spirit is that it usually recognizes and supports an idea as it appears in patterns of three. Most of all the One Spirit loves any good idea given freely and benevolently to others. The following exercise takes advantage of all these tendencies of spirit.

1. What is your desire? It could be for anything from personal peace, to healing, to some envisioned accomplishment. Refine the desire until you can select the perfect words that define it as near as you can. Now, say it out loud to yourself or write it down. Most importantly, express your feelings about it. Call up you inner passion about this particular subject. Feelings provide the energy for resonant attraction and harmony.

2. Next, find someone to listen to your desire and hold it with you. Together, see it accomplished. But, place no attachment as to how it will happen. Attachment can become an effort that pushes away the object of your desire.

3. The third step is vital. Envision a third person to whom you could give this desire and actually see it come to pass or be materialized. Envision how this could happen for another. Relax. See it accomplished. This is

66

actually the secret to how we keep our faith strong without holding on to limiting attachments. It also invokes the universal principle that as you give, so will you receive. It will happen for you now with much less effort than if you had held it only for yourself. Often it miraculously happens without delay!

4. Last but not least, be open to how your dreams and requests will be answered and provided for you. The Infinite spirit has ways, means, and connections of which we have not dreamed.

All of these steps are essential to refine the truth, faith, feeling, and benevolence of your goals. This process allows you to see your desire accomplished in detail without being blocked by your own past failures or fear of future failure. Remember, spirit has no failure and no resistance to any good thing especially when it can be shared and also held for the good of others.

Exercises for a more holy life:

1. See yourself in others. Let down your boundaries and separations. Enter a unified zone at least once a day, if only through expressions of joy.

2. Don't ask to be healed, but to be restored to that perfection from which you emanated.

3. Meditate. Much can be done in solitude when your focus is on elevating your energy level. One person on the earth at the energetic level of Christ or Buddha can alter the potential of history.

4. Discover the place within where prayer can alter your life and empower you to reach the very pinnacle of meditation – where no difference between prayer and meditation exists at all. In prayer you are offering the effects and affairs of your life for God for to elevate, disentangle, or heal. In meditation, we are listening for answers. By

disciplining our minds to be still, and allowing our hearts to open, we can foresee many greater possibilities for life. We become more unconditional, more tolerant, more receptive, and more open to the Creator's greater vision of how a prayer may best be answered and our life best be served.

Prayer

Divine Creator,
Give me the grace to see myself as you created me—
unflawed and able to know the true happiness of life.
Give me the clarity to see beyond my problems and to rise to heights
where I AM the solution.
Give me the strength to embrace my challenges with a spirit of adventure, knowing
that wherever I am, I am still with You.

Amen

My Personal Notes and Comments

70

Lesson 7

The Heart is Your Higher Intelligence

Our conversations about the heart were pivotal to all our discussions. He dwelt on it in great length, and frequently made mention of it to enhance the value of other subjects. To Jesus, the Sacred Heart holds the keys to the Kingdom of Heaven. *"The heart, which is your connecting link to God and the universe, integrates your own unique center of experience, awareness, and character with that which is beyond your comprehension."* Acceptance of that statement can only lead to the conclusion that the heart is our point of origin as well, the point from which we burst forth into life and by which our immortal continuance is sustained.

There is a great power within you, greater than the forces of fear or any of the blockages that might have been installed against your happiness. Huge bodies of evidence now confirm the existence of a vital link between our spirit, mind, body, and emotions. The following is a fascinating experiment conducted by the Institute of Heart Math. In this experiment, some human placenta DNA (the most pristine form of DNA) was placed in a container from which they could measure changes in the DNA. Twenty-eight vials of DNA were given (one each) to 28 trained researchers. Each researcher had been trained how to generate and FEEL feelings, and they each had strong emotions.

What was discovered was that the DNA CHANGED ITS SHAPE according to the feelings of the researchers: 1. When the researchers FELT gratitude, love and appreciation, the DNA responded by RELAXING and the strands unwound. The length of the DNA became longer. 2. When the researchers FELT anger, fear, frustration, or stress, the DNA responded by TIGHTENING UP. It became shorter and SWITCHED OFF many of our DNA codes! If you've ever felt "shut down" by negative emotions, this may explain why your body was equally shut down. The shutdown of the DNA codes was reversed and the codes were switched back on again when feelings of love, joy, gratitude and appreciation were felt by the researchers.

This experiment was later followed up by testing HIV positive patients. They discovered that feelings of love, gratitude, and appreciation created 300,000 TIMES the RESISTANCE they had without those feelings. Emotional input can go far beyond the effects of neurological signals to the body. Individuals trained in deep love were able to actually change the shape of their DNA. Essentially this report confirms that we influence our bodies and the whole web of creation through our emotional vibrations. [From a paper entitled: "Local and Non local Effects of Coherent Heart Frequencies & Conformational Changes of DNA."]

This experiment gives us substantial evidence that we create our reality by choosing it with our feelings! Our feelings activate our future and integrate it with the web of creation around us, which connects to all the energy and matter of the universe. Emotional and spiritual energy can cause profound changes in human performance. This energy is woven into a web surrounding your body, which connects with all matter, time, and space. The center of this web, on an individual level, is the human heart, and that marks the presence of an even more perfect center Jesus calls the Sacred Heart. In discovering this center you are acquiring access to the command center of your life where you will find answers to help you stay well, no matter what dreadful virus or bacteria may be floating around. By staying in feelings of joy, love, gratitude and appreciation your life will immeasurably improve!

Remember it is a universal law that our focus will activate or attract that to which we have given our energy. This can work to our benefit or to our detriment depending on whether our focus is on positive or negative issues. If you focus on fear of what may come, you are sending a strong message to the universe to provide you with exactly what you fear. It would be far better to open yourself to joy, love, appreciation or gratitude, and focus on bringing more of that into your life. In so doing, you will automatically avoid many negative manifestations.

According to Jesus, the Sacred Heart is the center of our personal universe. It is the magnetic force which attracts the effects of our life through the realities, feelings, and beliefs we feed to the heart. Whatever we place in the heart will be drawn back to us through its magnetic power. Our physical heart is the organ most perfectly created to facilitate and support an integration of body, mind, spirit, and emotions and to give command signals to your life. On some deep and subtle level (molecular or even atomic) the synchronization of all elements of your life is flawless and in perfect harmony with your reason for living. At this point the physical heart and the Sacred Heart are one. In that place you may receive the blessings of Heaven and pour them out onto the experiences of life.

At the same time, you must realize that this power magnifies **anything** you place in your heart. When I was a kid we had a mischievous little game of sticking signs to the back of another kid, unbeknownst to him of course, and on this sign we would write things like "pinch me" or "kiss me". When other kids plagued him or her with enough pinching or kissing (or whatever), he or she would begin to search for **why!** When the sign was finally discovered, we would all have a great laugh. I think of that game often when I consider all the signs I have placed unknowingly in my heart (or forgotten), and these signs have given instructions to life about what to dish out for me. Whenever I discover a hidden sign, I have a good laugh...but first I may have a good cry, because some of these signs may have caused unhappy experiences. So many people are looking for "signs" of the times... it would be well to first realize that the most powerful signs are in their hearts. These are the ones that will come true…and also the ones you can do something about.

There were many powerful revelations in 'Love Without End," and the most life-changing of all the teachings was about the Sacred Heart. In the years since the book was released, one of the most frequent questions asked by students is how to find and be in their Sacred Heart. The book offered several exercises for increasing one's awareness of the Sacred Heart, but if I were to add anything to those original teachings, it would be to emphasize that your Sacred Heart is IN YOU, not you in it! **It is your center.** From there, it is impossible to measure or quantify the outer reaches of all that you can be.

The Sacred Heart cannot be seen by ordinary perception. It cannot be fully apprehended through casual experience. To fully know the Sacred Heart is like the wedding night of your soul, which happens when we arrive in the place of pure being. Attaining this ultimate perception is not an easy task. It is virtually synonymous with realizing the presence of Christ within. Therefore, do not be impatient or harsh with yourselves. The good news is that every benchmark leading to awareness of the Sacred Heart is a wonderful place to be. Discoveries of the heart—be they physical or Sacred--can offer magnificent revelations about your inner power to change your life. Wherever you are in the journey, be assured the Sacred Heart is in you and with you. Celebrate its power at whatever level of reality is appropriate to your present understanding.

For purposes of your study here, I also want to encourage you to take your hearts lightly. Just because your heart is sacred, does not mean it is serious, somber, or only available for holy contemplations. The heart supports you in everything. Like a loving parent, it even indulges your folly and follows you into mischief rather than allowing you to suffer it alone. Your heart is the most adaptable and unconditional force within you. It is the center that never loses its centering. Perhaps, this is why it is often so hard to "find." The heart is a bit of a chameleon that changes colors in order to be with you in all things. This is comforting to know, and it is critical to realize as we study the heart's influence over our happiness.   By changing your heart, you can change your life... or the world.

"As a magnetic center, your heart is the great generator of all your life energy, and whenever you empower your heart you raise your energy level physically, mentally, emotionally, and spiritually."

Study Questions

1. What are the physiological components that allow your heart to be a "brain" in its own right?
2. What was the first cell and first organ created in your body?
3. Where is your personal "zero-point," and what does that mean?
4. What is indigenous power?   Give at least one example? By comparison, how does surrogate (delegated) power become a problem and under what conditions does it become a negative force? Give at least one example.
5. Where is the Sacred Heart to be found, and why is it there? What is the easiest, most natural way to enter into it.
6. Are words (and verbal prayers) necessary for entering the Sacred Heart?
7. When Jesus referred to the Kingdom of Heaven within, to what was he referring?
8. What is the symphonic universe, and how does it honor and preserve your presence and importance as a player in the symphony?
9. What are the levels of consciousness available to us, starting with bio-genetic and moving upward?
10. What are the seven dimensions of higher intelligence in the heart? Give examples of how each is represented in your own life and has guided your choices.

Exercises

Since the heart is your place of perfect synchronicity—body, feelings, spirit, and mind—it is particularly responsive to prayer and meditation. Like the heart, these practices are dedicated to higher states of peaceful, harmonic awareness. I find no better way of taking inventory of the heart, taking council from it, and also making needed changes than to spend time in prayer and meditation.

Investing a little time every day in quiet contemplations of the heart can result in attaining more harmony and removing more blocks to happiness than any other practice available to human consciousness. Prayer and meditation does for your state of consciousness what sleep does for your body. When you restore your relationship with the heart, you bring immense vitality into your life. Many problems will simply dissolve into the harmony of higher living.

Heart Breath

I will now teach you a very special breath that helps to integrate body spirit, emotions, and all levels of consciousness in the heart center of your body. Some of you have learned this in seminars with me, and I learned it so long ago I am not sure who I learned it from. But, it has served me well in developing a harmonious and conscious relationship with my heart. There are never too many occasions to practice and apply this powerful breath.

Special breathing has been used in prayer, meditation, and sacred disciplines of the body since time immemorial because breath is the perfect symbol of life. Our lives began with breath, and without it life would end immediately. Breath is also the most effective symbol we have for the presence of spirit in physical form. In the book of Genesis, it is said that God breathed His spirit into man and man came to life.

The physical heart is our vital organ responsible for transforming breath into the substances of life. This special "heart breath" is designed to heighten this function. In so doing, it will stimulate all the functions of the physical heart as well as the spiritual center that it also serves.

First I will describe this breath. Then I will coach you through it. This will start with a deep, full breath that focuses on expanding the center of your chest where your physical heart is located. The heart breath varies from other types of deep breathing, which have their emphasis on cleansing the lungs by taking large quantities of fresh air into the deepest recesses of your lungs and then forcing all of the old stale air out. **This breathing exercise is different.** In the heart breath you will be expanding and contracting your lungs in the **center** of your chest in order to make intentional physical contact with your heart and give it a loving, nurturing massage! This also assists the muscles surrounding and supporting your heart to relax and to let your heart know that there is a larger network of support for it to draw upon. You will be giving your heart a rich supply of oxygen while you are expressing your deep support and appreciation for its ceaseless work. As you breathe in, offer your heart new positive feelings, words, affirmations, and beliefs. As you breath out, release old negative feelings, self-defeating words, and negative beliefs.

So, let's begin. Find a comfortable quiet position. You do not have to close your eyes or assume a meditative pose, but be prepared to give your heart your full loving attention. Once you become masterful with this breath, you can do it anytime, anywhere. It can be used to create greater relaxation or alertness or whatever condition supports your heart in having greater command of life. Inhale deeply to about the count of five or six. The number is not important, except that you learn to create the optimum **full breath for you,** one that is paced to a medium rhythm. It is aerobic and invigorating but not short and panting. Nor is it so slow and deep that it has no aerobic impact. Feel your chest expanding, and your shoulder blades gently spreading out from your spine. Now exhale to that same count (about five or six). Feel your chest relaxing and your shoulders falling. Be very regular and controlled in your rhythm, but focus on the nurturing energy it is providing for your heart. Create this breath **around your heart!** Imagine that the act of expanding and contracting your lungs is massaging your heart. Allow your heart to enjoy being fully supported by your attention and intention. Now, focus on your out-breath and begin to release negative perceptions or beliefs, such as "I'm so tired", or "I'll never get through this" or "I'll never find the answer." You can eventually start releasing deeper, life-long negative feelings, beliefs, and decisions. In the next step, change your focus to the in-breath and supply your heart with the beliefs and feelings you want. These might include, "there's always enough," or "I'll find the answer," or "my friends will be there for me." Finally, express your love and appreciation for your heart and its sacred connection to God and all forms of your higher guidance. Then receive your heart's undying love for you. Enjoy the results. This simple exercise will make a profound difference in your ability to be in positive alignment with the highest and best for your life.

Now that your heart is energized and refreshed with your loving attention, this would be a good time to practice the manifesting technique that I gave you in Chapter 5. This is a simple, but profound technique for discovering, defining, and achieving your desires. The best part is that it reveals how much your heart attracts and God provides your desires without having to apply any external motivation. I would like to quote a passage from *"The Keys of Jeshua"* that will strengthen your understanding.

> *"The desires of the heart are not directed toward seeking that which you do not have or toward attaining that which is inappropriate for your life. Your heart sees beyond the illusions of insufficiency, for it knows the greater truth that everything you ever will have has already been given. The sacred heart of your being knows no sense of lack except to fulfill its relationship with God. The desire of your heart is to discover the hiding places of your wealth, and to make you joyful enough to receive it. Equal to*

that is its expression of gratitude for what you already have, including that which has not yet been attained or received. It is the pleasure of the heart to make you ready for your treasure.

"Do not be fooled by illusions of neediness which only make you more thirsty. Instead, strengthen your love by giving thanks for that which is yet unborn, and by singing praise even if the pain of life would make you cry.

"The game of life is to pierce the illusion of need. There is a special reality within every soul that contains a seed for growth and eventual harvest. As you cultivate this gift with love and faith, your heart will discern your bounty and unfold it in your life.

"You could not even conceive of that which has not already been planted in your soul as an eventual reality. So when you pray, do so in joy for that which has been promised and pray for guidance that your mind may work in harmony with your heart, to direct your life toward its fulfillment. Whenever you do this, you strengthen both your faith and your integrity to know and attune your life to that which is truly yours. When you seek and pursue that which is not truly yours, you will develop a kind of hunger that cannot be appeased, and a deep sense of 'neediness', which distorts your life and creates dis-ease." (The Keys of Jeshua, Chapter 5, p. 57)

Seeing Paradise

There are many dimensions of the heart. There are those that provide a basis for our higher intelligence and provide us with the energy for our manifesting our dreams. There is also the most sacred inner place where we commune with God and have contact to alone with our own immortal self. This is the Kingdom of Heaven within which Jesus called the Sacred Heart. Therefore, I give you one last exercise for strengthening your ability to enter and feel the Sacred Heart. Like any ability, this will grow with practice.

Assume a meditative pose. Close your eyes and relax your body. Now let your mind release its dense accumulations of thought like dropping a stone into deep still cool water. Watch the stone fall to the bottom of the lake of water and see eddies expanding out to infinity. Next, ask yourself, "What does Paradise look like to me?" Using your powers of visualization, like you would do if you were dreaming, begin to create the images of Paradise. Don't worry if you can't make them look fully real and solid. The most important thing is that you FEEL the elements of Paradise and have a sense of being attracted to them. Whatever comes forth in your paradise, don't judge. Notice the feelings, and all the other souls that come to join you. Just let it happen. Enjoy. Once you feel immersed in that experience select just one scene from your current place in life. With the same kind of imagination, create that situation just outside the energy of Paradise. From inside Paradise, view that current life situation and see how it changes. Accept whatever is being revealed. You may repeat this part of the process with as many situations as you wish, but end off while you are still refreshed and enlivened from the energy of Paradise. As you grow proficient in this, it will help you to be more effective IN the world, and also to know beyond a shadow of a doubt that you are not OF the world. Before or after this meditation you may want to say this prayer.

Prayer

I praise you, O Infinite God of all life,
All existence, and all goodness.
I thank you for sharing your life, and goodness,
So freely with me and making me one with you.

Help me to discover and nurture the treasure
You have already given, that I may find my place
Within your rich abundance.

Teach me to respect the evolving nature of all creation,
That I may see every day as the answer to a prayer
And every prayer as the faith I pledge
For the coming of a new day.

Amen

My Personal Notes and Comments

Lesson 8

Bridges

As we open the pages of this lesson I would like to suggest that every bridge presents us with a hint of purpose, a reason for its existence. After all, bridges are connecting extensions providing safe passage from one side of a chasm to the other. A bridge is a potent symbol, and Jesus said, "You are a bridge." You are a bridge from the Divine Creator into continuing creation. Perhaps to be a bridge is sufficient purpose once we understand how to explore, use, develop, and honor the importance of bridges for the furtherance of life. At the same time, our own sense of purpose is the most powerful bridge we have for arriving at our ultimate fulfillment.

From "The Keys of Jeshua" there is this very relevant teaching about purpose which will lead you into a deeper understanding of what he means by "bridges." This excerpt will also provide some valuable links with your preceding lessons about your Heart's intelligence and the One Spirit.

> *"One purpose is not more important than another. What elevates one purpose over another is the dedication you make to it, the value of it to others, and the satisfaction it brings to you. There*

are two major blocks to seeing your purpose more clearly, and both are very common in today's world.

"The first is lack of self-esteem. That condition is always a challenge to the discovery of purpose, because purpose is what grants meaning to your life... from the inside out. When you feel unworthy to know your value to others, you will block your purposes. You cannot have deep and enduring satisfaction unless you have self-worth. This is one reason why work, service, and contribution all help in preparing you to know your purpose.

"The second block is a loss of the sacred. Purpose is the recognition of the sacred within us. That realization will lead you to a choice of work that is in harmony with sacred presence. It may find expression through family, community, relationships, work, creative pursuits, and practices of faith.

"...Purpose is like the mountain that connects heaven to earth. Through pathways up the mountain, man can raise himself to the divine, and through such sincere effort, the divine can reveal itself to man. For many people, this pathway up the mountain is through nature and all things natural. For others, it is through creativity and intuitive exploration. For some, it is through work and human service. For others, it is through spiritual, ethical, or intellectual discipline. For all, it is through some measure of faith and explorations of the heart.

"Discovery of purpose is a continuous pursuit, rewarded by an endless procession of revelations. We each live this process every day as we listen to life and shape our destiny. If there were any shortcuts to finding your purpose they would consist of establishing priorities, dedication, and satisfaction; and most of all, joy." (The Keys of Jeshua, p. 241-242)

In the simplest terms a bridge is just a progression that takes us from one place to another, whether it is up a mountain or across a gorge. In order to expedite our goals and aspirations in life, it is important to understand the way in which our bridges are built, and with what ingredients.

84

As you move through this lesson I recommend many diagrams about your life in which you literally draw bridges from one condition to another and identify the necessary parts of the bridges that will take you to your desired destination. A bridge could be as simple as acquiring more understanding about a subject or issue, as pivotal as finding just the right connection, or as complex as formulating a plan for complete change of life. In each case, there is a logical progression (carried by a sense of purpose). Jesus has revealed the anatomy of that progression in Chapter 8.

So often we want a quick trip to the other side, to fly across the chasm. But, what we do not understand is that the process of getting there is essential to the goal and its attainment. These teachings will contribute greatly to the ease, confidence, and clarity with which you make all future progressions in life, whether they are spiritual or material.

> We will not be so impatient when we understand that the process and the achievement are inseparable.

Study Questions

This is a lesson more aptly served by your answers to the well-directed questions.

1. What does Jesus mean by "bridges?"
2. Does intelligence begin with the mind or something even more basic?
3. Thoughts, ideas, and concepts are crystallizations of _____?
4. How did symbols and language develop from basic awareness?
5. Why is it that the heart can change your life when your mind can only rearrange it? How does this relate to the power of intention?
6. What is the difference between will and intention?

7. How does thought create a parallel experience for us that allows us to examine our life and the consequences of what we are considering?
8. How is cause and effect a predictable bridge from today to tomorrow?
9. How are your beliefs a bridge to connect unborn potential with manifest reality? How do belief 'systems' often become disconnected with reality?
10. What are the elements of prophesy? Include examples of positive and wise prophesy as well as negative and manipulative prophesy. Show examples of how you have been your own prophet, both in terms of visionary foresight and self-fulfilling negative projections.
11. What does Jesus mean by fluid reality?

Study Exercises

1. Describe the progression from general awareness to a well-formed thought. Show at least one example in your own life.
2. Describe at least one example in your own life of the maxim, "as you connect so you think, and as you think so you connect?"
3. Consider how you could be a bridge for God's will to come into activation.
4. Find at least one area in your life where progressive improvements could eventually make a huge difference.
5. Write a paragraph (or longer) on how you are a bridge from heaven to earth.

Prayer

O Divine Creator,
Reveal your presence within me that I may know the
Purpose for which I was created.

Fill me with creativity so that I may bear the
Fruit of your will.
Grant me the wisdom to produce and share
Whatever is truly of service.
Keep me on the path of true purpose.
Help me to discover the rich opportunity of
Each present moment.
For you are the ground of my being and the
Power of my fulfillment.
You are the joy in my work, and the
Peace that calls me to rest when day is done.
In you, I am made whole again.

Amen

My Personal Notes and Comments

Lesson 9

The Blessed Life

Is it possible to enjoy Heaven on Earth? Why do we think of Paradise being far away from mortal struggles and worldly existence? Under the relentless pressures of survival we often dream of kinder, gentler places and seek to escape into the shelter of worlds beyond. Yet, Jesus said the Kingdom of Heaven is within us and is available through the very process of living.

So, what is the roadmap? What is the secret? Where is the bridge? Jesus made an amazing assertion when he said the answers were all in the Beatitudes.

Personally, one of the most pronounced changes I have noticed in myself through applying his teaching is the way I deal with problems. I have always enjoyed challenges and have often received very pleasant adrenaline rushes from successfully rising to an occasion. I am convinced that I have attracted many, if not most, of the contests in my life because of the experience and accomplishment they provided. In retrospect, I have to admit that problem solving has often provided my ego with a victory in some illusionary way! Ironically, I have finally learned that the real victory is returning to the bliss of who I truly am—no matter what-- knowing that I can attain repose **independently** of external conditions.

Along with that, I have found many difficult conditions are simply expendable by choice.

The purpose of this chapter is to help you receive all the blessings of life and to spot and release your blockages to happiness and fulfillment.

Even those who feel happy and well most of the time are nonetheless held hostage by unseen internal forces that limit their full experience of life. Most of these forces do not exist outside your selves, and there is nothing negative or sinister about them. They are simply part of your on-going challenge to awaken and grow. This kind of growth begins by realizing that true blessings are unconditional. Despite the appearance of challenge, there are actually no obstacles to overcome... other than your allowance to acknowledge and accept your blessings as a gift from God.

Perhaps the greatest gift of all is our natural state of joy, for it allows us to receive all the other blessings without asking 'why' or needing to justify them. In its purest form, joy is simply unconditional. Joy is our greatest emotional friend, because it teaches us to take ourselves less seriously. Joy also works on our behalf to dissolve the blockages we place on success and happiness as well as our fear of failure.

True joy is our native state, providing we do not blind ourselves to its presence. Unlike happiness, which we strive to achieve, joy wells up from within and is often irrelevant to external circumstances. We can even have a disconcerting sense of joy in the midst of painful events where logic and appropriateness might post a sign saying "no joy permitted." In such times of pain or sorrow, where grief is a more fitting expression, we often deny or squelch our feelings of joy, out of guilt and confusion. What we fail to realize is that joy is a love letter from God reminding us of our true spiritual nature, which is greater than any difficult circumstance.

We are often reluctant to admit finding joy in challenging situations. Perhaps this is because we are made anxious by such illogical appearances of it. More likely, we are afraid that in accepting our inner reserves of joy we are also accepting or endorsing the pain in which we found it. Perhaps we need to realize that we are not reduced by those moments of hardship, no more than we are elevated by other moments of predictable pleasure.   All the panorama of life is spread before us as a banquet. Through our inner reserves of joy it can all be redeemed as a blessing.

The spontaneous, unconditional, irrepressible fountain of joy within you has the power to unlock every inhibition to happiness and aliveness... without looking any further for answers. It is also the most direct pathway to knowing your love. In the words of Jesus:

"The truest way to know your love is not by reflection but by the joy you feel in its presence. That joy is the soul's pleasure in the presence of love. Whatever you experience as joy is the cup of your love overflowing. By your joy you shall know your love, and the nature of your soul, as it casts your love upon the waters of life."

"Only when you love beyond all of the external conditions which logically tell you not to do so, can you discover the deeper wellspring of love that you are. In the twenty-third chapter of the Book of Psalms, King David welcomes the Lord to set a table before him in the presence of his enemies, knowing that his cup will be filled to overflowing. His cup was filled with love. David knew that only through the power of love could victory be attained. **Through love you have the power over any**

91

situation. Only, you will never truly know this until you have surmounted adversity. The last of the beatitudes is the greatest of all blessings. For in that learning, you are free forever from the illusions that would attempt to conquer you and misdirect your life."

Joy is an inner force, sustaining with us on the paths of life and direct us toward our blessings. Joy lifts us to a higher perspective and disperses illusion while counseling us with patience to pause and restore the love that we are. It simply remarks at what is happening, without judgment, position, or inhibition. Thus, we have accessed a higher power, which transcends all the conditions, judgments, and inhibitions we place on our lives... good, bad, happy, sad.

When we read the Beatitudes as they have traditionally been presented (or misinterpreted) we do not always see the foundation of joy that empowers each one. Therefore, we will review each of them from that higher perspective, including joy as the internal power which sustains, guides, and lifts us to a fuller life:

1. *Blessed are the poor in spirit for theirs is the Kingdom of Heaven.* This is the blessing of simplicity and transcendence over complications in life. Just consider the joy that brings.
2. *Blessed are those that mourn, for they will be comforted.*
   This is the blessing of release that allows us to partake in the joy of change. Even though letting go can be painful, this is the "other side" of love that prepares us for receiving again. It is a kind of birthing pain for new love.
3. *Blessed are the meek for they will inherit the earth.* This is the blessing that assures us all things must be kept in balance. By keeping the balance ourselves, we have great joy in knowing there will be no unkind surprises about how the universe restores its balance toward us.
4. *Blessed are those who hunger and thirst for righteousness, for they will be filled.* This is the joy of advancing our hearts and consciousness toward the light of God.

5. *Blessed are the merciful, for they will receive mercy.* This is the joy of using our strength and authority wisely and benevolently. In so doing, we have the further joy of knowing that we will be given even greater authority and strength.

6. *Blessed are the pure in heart, for they shall see God.* This is the joy of discovering that sacred place within where we may commune with God.

7. *Blessed are the peacemakers, for they shall be called sons of God.* Who does not enjoy peace, but how much more joy do we have when we have understanding of our place in it and have an understanding of how to sustain it.

8. *Blessed are those who are persecuted for righteousness sake, for theirs is the Kingdom of Heaven.* This is the joy of setting one's soul and one's integrity above all earthly challenges. This is undoubtedly, the most difficult lesson in attaining the blessed life. As creatures seeking pleasure and avoiding pain, it is very difficult to resolve our most basic instinct with that ultimate realization. This is where our minds and all lower drives will fall by the wayside. In this blessing our hearts are restored to supreme command. This is the blessing that promises our ultimate transcendence from the hardships of life. It also has a second profound realization to offer:

"There is a second meaning to this beatitude which teaches us how to vanquish negative illusions. This begins with realizing that 'for righteousness sake' means 'for love's sake.' Whenever you stand firmly in the midst of a hardship, holding and expressing the love that you are, you will witness illusions falling away. Through being the love that you are, you are empowered to transcend your sufferings."

Jesus said to me more than once, *"Love your enemies if you would convince yourself that love is a power that comes from within."*

Perhaps there are no enduring enemies, but there are adversarial situations. Life has its trials, and when we are passing through these difficulties it is imperative to be the love that we are. In that special state of being, we gain the assurance that we are not externally controlled or dominated by the world.

"Only in the presence of your enemy can you really discover that truth. Only when you love beyond all of the external conditions which logically tell you not to do so, can you discover the deeper wellspring of love that you are."

Study Questions:

1. What is the relationship between structure and separation?
2. What are the two phases of love?
3. How does mourning differ from grieving?
4. What is God's economy?
5. What establishes true ownership?
6. What does Jesus mean by "when you are merciful, you grow?"
7. How does God's redemption differ from judgment?

Study Exercises:

1. Examine your life to see where you have made decisions about the value of challenges and hardships.
2. Examine your life to see where there are already little pieces of Heaven on Earth. Express gratitude for these, and hold them as evidence of even greater things that are possible.
3. Write each one of the Beatitudes again **in your own words according to how you see them apply to your life.** Give yourself at least one example of how each one has already blessed your life. State an intention of how you may apply each principle to present and future situations in life.

My Personal Notes and Comments

Lesson 10

The Ten Commandments of Love

The essence of this chapter is about the way love and the pursuit of truth form the basis for living a decent, productive, and fulfilling life.

For most of us these principles are so deeply etched in our character that they are expressed in subtle combinations every day as just being a decent, caring human being. Because of this, we often give little thought to the component elements of the forces behind them, which actually govern our lives.

In this chapter we have an opportunity to examine the nature of universal law, ethics, and morality as never before, because in Jesus' teaching they all have a common foundation, namely love. Yet each one has a different application in life.

Laws pertain to the workability of our universe. Keeping things working as intended is what law is all about. Ethics is the creation and establishment of values in life and in our shared communities. Morality is the way we maintain our integrity and self-esteem in the flow of life as according in support of shared life and our need to get along with others. Morality is more about the agreements we make among ourselves as to acceptable conduct. Unfortunately, in our human arrogance we often promote moral codes to the status of law, after which they become

97

ridged, stagnant, and eventually obsolete. For example in the United States only a hundred years ago it was immoral for a lady to wear trousers unless her work required it. In some countries today it is immoral for a woman to appear in public with her head uncovered. Jesus said that morality must always keep pace with our need for growth and change, in its highest form it is change for the better. Morality directly relates to our power of choice. When we are moral, we choose goodness for ourselves and others. What 'goodness' means can be highly relative is different situations. However, the essence of morality is that we chose betterment, at least as we see it.

> *Laws are to maintain the natural and essential order of existence. Ethics are for the development and implementation of values. Morality is for sharing of life with agreements that serve the greater good of all.*

These three guidelines for conduct have one thing in common...love. In real life they are usually interwoven and often confused. By 'combing them out' and seeing each strand in a unique light, however, we can achieve much clarification about judgment and how conflicts can arise just in the process of being a good person. So let's take a closer look at each of these categories of optimal conduct.

Universal law: Love is the law in our universe and truth is the constant. All other laws derive their power from that. Because of that: *"The laws which serve God are revealing and transformative, always in an upward direction. Law is to support life, and correct it where necessary. A society which uses law only as a platform for judgment will fall into peril. Law has no validity in itself except through the love in which it is rooted. Love's power does not replace nor override the workable laws of conduct. Love exposes the reasons for law, replacing enforcement with true enlightenment."*

In distinction from ethics and morality, however, "law" is a constant power in all conditions, which carries its mandate without respect of persons. On the physical, mechanical level, the law of gravity would be a

98

good example. No one argues with gravity, and when it claims it toll no one takes it personally. Why is it then that we try to out-maneuver the laws of love? Partly, I think, because we confuse them with the other two categories of good conduct which are indeed context relevant and subject to free will. Those topics are ethics and morality, and even they are often confused, so let's look for some clarity. According to Jesus: *"Ethics is the ongoing process of applying principles of higher intelligence to the problems of personal collective existence, and endowing life with values that support the well-being of all. Ethics is the care we show in affecting the lives of others as well as a sense for where one's greatest value lies in relation to others. Ethics might be summarized as cause and effect in balance, and applied for the greatest good. Ethics is value based."*

Our values say a lot about us, what we hold dear and what we most seek. As we live, gain experience, and gain a better understanding of how to live together and cooperatively with nature, our values evolve. Our values are directly affected by our understanding and education, and most especially by the wisdom of our hearts. These are the standards by which we work, live, play, and share life with others. They cannot be enforced, and must be held by choice.

Morality is the most personal of our codes of conduct, and ironically (at least in the past), the one most subject to societal enforcement. I personally feel that one of the causes of our society's loose morality today is that we have relaxed societal enforcement while failing to see the personal component of morality, which is one's desire for personal integrity.

"Morality is oriented toward decency, kindness, and improvement. It is essentially the devotion we have to bring about change for the better. Morality involves a responsibility for the situations that arise in life and the willingness to confront them honestly and deal with them directly to cause an improvement. Part of this involves the personal hygiene of body, mind, emotions, thought, and spirit. Cleanliness is indeed next to Godliness. Morality, however, is a personal attainment. It cannot be enforced externally without weakening the 'I Am' presence of an individual.

99

"Ethics is imperative for social decency and a workable civilization. Morality is imperative for personal clarity, strength, and virtue. The simplicity of it all, though, is that both are rooted in love."

Study Questions:

1. What is the relationship of the first commandment to establishing correct priorities?
2. What is the relationship between the Sabbath and the resting points in various rhythms? What does this have to do with pacing our lives with purpose and intentional grace?
3. How does acknowledgment and appreciation of contexts contribute to honorable living?
4. What is the relationship between justice and abundance? How does this shed new light on the damaging nature of scarcity?
5. What other powers of life can be "killed" other than one's physical body?
6. What does Jesus mean by adulteration in a relationship and how does it eventually lead to adultery?
7. What is the true law of property?
8. What is the relationship between the ninth commandment and innocent perception?
9. How does truly being yourself provide simple and complete remedy to the tenth commandment?

Study Exercises:

1. Take each one of the commandments and put it into your own words as it seems most real to you. Leave plenty of space for additional comments between each commandment.

Recall at least one time when honoring that law made a profoundly positive effect in your life.

Recall at least one time when someone else honoring that law made a profoundly positive effect in your life.

Recall at least one time when either you or someone else disregarded that law and undesirable effects resulted.

Look at your values and see how they have a direct correlation with your service to others and that which you hope to receive from others.
Look at the guidelines by which you maintain your personal integrity. According to Jesus, this is your true standard of morality.

My Personal Notes and Comments

Lesson 11

Your Rights and Freedoms

This is one of my favorite chapters in the book. I gain such freedom and joy each time I read it. Actually, if it were not for the chronology of events and some essential basics that needed to be explained first, I would have made it the beginning chapter of the book. That may seem like a shocking statement, but the assurances of this chapter have everything to do with your right to know the messages of *"Love Without End"* and to make your own choices about how to use it in your life. This chapter contains the basic tenants of your own right to grow in Christ Consciousness, and to pursue your own personal and spiritual elevation as an inalienable right given by God.

*"Free will is the foundation right given by the Holy Father to all of His children. It is the right to be who you really are and to make choices in life which give evidence to that truth. Life is full of movement, with varying possibilities and options for change. Through the choices you make, you give support to your life, your love, and your truth. In and of itself, a context or environment may or may not honor or sustain the essence of who you are. The reason is that you are a child of God and **not** a child of circumstance. The very fact of having free will is what liberates you from*

*the imprisonment of circumstance. You may initiate changes to make a situation compatible with your love, and you can choose not to support those situations that deny your love. Even if none of the choices available to you is ideal, the **very act of making choices** will give you an assertive power over external conditions and a way of moving through them."*

My recommendation is that you make every right discussed in this chapter your guiding light in all that you do. There is nothing that can bring positive focus and eliminate distraction and negative drain more efficiently than just following these prescriptions for free will.

It has been mentioned in several other contexts that free will is the absolute right given by God to all souls. Because we do not know this consciously, assuming full responsibility for it, many hardships and misdeeds have occurred. There is possibly nothing more important in our spiritual growth and evolution of consciousness than to gain a full understanding of these freedoms that have been given to all.

In seminars I always receive questions about why, if we are all love, there are so many violent and criminal actions in the world. The answer to that is free will. Without free will, our choice of love and goodness would be meaningless. In that very question and answer, you can see the importance of this topic for our spiritual mastery. As a central part of our growth we have to first realize that everything is a choice given to us, and then take the further step to learn the responsibility of having been given the freedom of choice.

The good news is that you always have the right to choose love, regardless of your conditions, circumstances, or past actions. In my opinion, this is why forgiveness is so important—forgiveness for oneself and others. Because forgiveness releases the past negative conditioning that prevails on our mind's tendency to look for predictable patterns and to repeat what has come before.

You can't fake it though. Forgiveness must be genuine. There must be true release. This is freedom from the past. As Jesus said, forgiveness boggles the mind and opens up possibilities unforeseen without it. Forgiveness invites new opportunities for choice. So does tolerance and loving allowance. Whenever more choices are available, the odds increase that love will be chosen. After all, it is the natural tendency of a child of God regardless of his past.

Above all, enjoy this chapter. Savor every right for the trust, confidence, esteem, and joy that Divine Providence has vested in you!

Study Questions:

1. What does it mean where Jesus says that "rights belong to the individual and not the condition?"
2. What does it mean where Jesus says that all souls are not only endowed with equal rights by their Creator, but also they have the same right to be respected even in their unequal conditions?
3. How does judgment interfere with the exercise of your rights and those of others?
4. What is the one condition for entering the Sacred Heart? How can you attain the condition easily?
5. How do imagination and creativity take you beyond structure?
6. Why does most suffering occur? Look for examples in your own life.
7. What is the relationship between making choices and being creative?
8. How do you get honest answers?

9. What is the sole intent of judgment? Apply this to your experience of everyone who has ever judged you.
10. What is the last judgment?

Study Exercises:

1. Read this quote again carefully:

*"How your eternal life unfolds is entirely according to your love. Where your love is, there will you be also. **I do not say this casually. It is the law. As your love is, so will you be.** When your love has refined itself to prefer and enjoy Heavenly pleasures, then you will be there. For those who love the seamier side of life, there will be a domain where that aspect of life is made available to you. Wherever your love is, there you will be. Your love cannot be stopped, and you will be with it. Love brings your lessons, friends, blessings, and opportunities. All of your patterns of growth, and all of the changes in your life have come about because something changed in the pattern of your love. It is through developing patterns of love that change unfolds in your life. You are not going to have your love in one place and be somewhere else!*

"Your love walks hand and hand with your immortality. In knowing this you will have confidence that fulfillment is truly possible. It begins by realizing that your life extends well beyond any structures that would bind you ... even to the point of immortality. This is your right."

Look at how love has brought you to every situation in your life, even if it was indirectly channeled through other motivations and beliefs about what you were doing. Love is even above belief. Love survives and directs even the darkest and most challenging passages of our life. It is essential that you become conscious of how love has worked in your life. Then you can acknowledge and accept its power to manifest your circumstances. Only then can you bless and accept those support persons and systems that still serve you, and release those that have completed their time with you. It is essential that you maintain your free will even with love. Even though we embrace our responsibilities, love must not be a burden or depleting obligation.

2. Look over your life. Express appreciation for everything you have experienced and how it has brought you greater understanding or resolution. Now examine any feeling you have about your life being inadequate or not having certain experiences that others have had. Let go of all feelings that have no value to you. Re-read page 234 where Jesus explains that you do not have to experience everything to have a complete life. Look then at how you can use the rest of your life to experience that which you love instead of questing for that which is irrelevant to you.

3. Look at how you deal with situations where your personal realities are different from external realities. Do you become defensive, annoyed, deflated, or insecure? Or, do you remain confident that you have the right to a personal reality as long as you respect that right for others and also carefully study the terrain of your common reality? What can you do to become less polarized or apprehensive when differences of reality happen between you and others close to you?

My Personal Notes and Comments

Lesson 12

God and Reality

We have a marvelously workable, elegant universe that can meet our every need and fulfill our every desire if we will only learn and apply its truth to our perception of reality. The universe got here before we did. Yes, we humans have a privileged relationship with the Creator, but we were also the last ones invited to the party. Even the animals arrived before we did. This is not to suggest that we are anything other than indigenous to the whole of everything. We have been given the privilege of co-creation and even the right to create our own personal reality. Indeed, we have. The point I want to make is that we are inheritors who need to acknowledge and respect the clay from which we shape the vessels of our lives. In that clay is the body of God and it contains miraculous potential.

The complexity of this chapter is directly in proportion to the density of our misconceptions about God being somewhere else, and the clay of physical substance being inert and lifeless until it conforms to OUR reality.

The truth is, everything you touch is alive as energy, and once you understand all the progressions it has undergone from God the Source to being God the vessel you can find a way of relating to it that empowers your hopes and dreams. You are very loved ... or you would not be here. That is a given. Therefore, the universe is completely ready to support you, but on **mutual** terms. It is ready to support the love that you are created in the image of God and to honor your free will and creations. At the same time we are expected to grow in the knowledge that our planet and universe are the vessels of God, which have their own terms and character. Exposing this actuality and mutuality, and helping you to use it profitably for your happiness and expansion, is the purpose of this chapter.

In our scientifically driven, materialistic western society we think of truth as that which can be verified and confirmed by study and evidence. We see it as "that which is," or that which is waiting to be discovered and revealed. We see it as that which can be witnessed and confirmed from all angles of evidence, as in our jurisprudence system. Yet we must ask how many tenants of belief have been confused for truth? Such as the world is flat, that there is a far edge in the ocean over which none shall survive. That the sun revolves around the earth. Even by the most legitimate standards of scientific study and proof, how many supposed "truths" have been revised with a change of perspective? One that comes to mind is Isaac Newton's various laws of classical physics that have been explained differently, though not overturned, by the laws of quantum physics. And, I wonder, what new and greater perspective will revise and make adjustments to quantum physics.

In our own personal lives and experience, how often have we needed to correct an early conclusion that we considered to be true after further evidence was provided? How many times have we had to learn that something we believed in sincerely was only a belief and not the truth? I feel this is the fundamental reason that Jesus emphasized the importance of faith beyond than that of belief. Faith is measured by the strength of our connection with God through which all things we do not yet understand can still be held to and claimed in full realization when the time is right.

Jesus was always careful to point out that we are collectively building our consciousness and reality. In relation to the larger specter of reality we are all like "blind men" touching some part of the proverbial elephant, and then attempting to construct the whole by comparing observations. The redeeming aspect of this is the presence of truth within all reality. Therefore, when we compare our experiences, if they are honestly reported, they will provide us with some part of the truth we seek.

Reality is as diverse as our perception of it, or our considerations about it, so how do we find truth within reality? Jesus said God is one with reality, but sometimes reality is so harsh and confusing. How do we keep our balance within it and feel the presence of God?

> *"God is one with reality and man has been chosen as the heir and extender of that reality. Do you think that He does not care whether you rise up to that fulfillment? As you demonstrate your* **zest for reality***, you will be met more than half way with love, support, and assistance that will seem nothing short of miraculous to you.*
>
> *"Your life on earth is to build faith and consciousness. As you do that, you will find that reality is both a comfort and a miracle. Until you know that simple truth, you will mistakenly seek your comfort through structure, your miracles through illusion, and your competence through specialization. This is the state of separation that most men and women experience."*

Truth is not so much a "thing" as a window, a doorway, which unveils the constants by which a greater Presence can be known. Truth is the answer your soul is seeking. The answer does not lie in data, experience, beliefs, or pushing the boundaries of reality. What you **do** need is a better understanding of how and where to **find** the truth.

The answer we're looking for lies at the core of our being. At the core of your being you will be able to evaluate life experiences from an axial center point rather than a boundary-based context. If you have studied any form of science at any level, you will know that defining the context is absolutely essential to making all the other determinations. In the past almost every context was drawn or described by its boundaries. The boundary WAS the context. Now we have a new definition of "context." Most studies now define a context by its center, with probabilities for expansion and influence or surrounding conditions, yet with its constant at the center. A higher definition of any context can be determined from its center rather than its boundaries. Knowing this is freedom in both thinking and being, for it will dissolve boundaries and polarities.

> "The primal constants of the universe are free of time and space, and therefore reveal the height and depth of consciousness. Truth transcends reality and distills it into simple understanding! It is truth that sets you free from the limiting aspects of dependencies and conditions.
> "Far from being a pillar of stone, truth is both dynamic and evolving. It reveals itself as you discover the constants within your being and your experience. Truth is the power of constancy that allows you to experience growth and change without being anything other than your own 'true' self. Truth is what allows experimentation and examination of reality to occur (which innately changes the object of study) yet reveals a reliable constant that can be measured, verified, and reliably used in other contexts. LWE, Chapter 12, p. 292

If Truth is the constant we find within the universe and our experience of it, what is it within our self that is capable of connecting with truth and realizing it for our own benefit? What is our constant? Even if we can grasp and embrace the idea that love is who we are, is that not ever growing and changing? What is the mysterious connection we have to the truth within, the truth revealed, the truth expressed?

I think *that answer comes in just one word: Light.*

It was said about Jesus in the Gospels:

> *Mt 28:3 His form was shining like the light, and his clothing was white as snow:*

112

Joh 8:12 Then again Jesus said to them, I am the light of the world; he who comes with me will not be walking in the dark but will have the light of life.

And what about after such time as he no longer is walking the earthly paths? How shall the light be given? There is an amazing suggestion that the torch shall be passed to any of us who will ignite the candle within our own soul:

Mt 5:14 You are the light of the world. A town put on a hill may be seen by all.
Mt 5:15 And a burning light is not put under a vessel, but on its table; so that its rays may be shining on all who are in the house.
Mt 5:16 Even so let your light be shining before men, so that they may see your good works and give glory to your Father in heaven.

In the next chapter of Matthew there is a potent connection between "seeing the truth" and lighting the fire within:

Mt 6:22 The light of the body is the eye; if then your eye is true, all your body will be full of light.

Those who have achieved enlightenment call it that for good reason. It is not incidental that the most common response to some new or regained realization is, "I see." One of the great similarities of light and consciousness is that they both create **and** result from conditions of integration, order, and harmony.

In the Book of Genesis we are told that the first act of creation was light. In the Book of John we are told that in the beginning was The Word, meaning Logos or consciousness. Are light and logos the same? Everything I have discovered about the wholeness of life seems to indicate they are. We cannot encompass the entirety of God, but we can walk in the light of a Higher Consciousness.

In all of creation, light was the first manifestation of Being. Before there was light there was a void (nothing). In all references to it, both spiritually and physically, light is the constant of **all that is.** Light always refers to Being and never to nothing, or even to doing. Even when we flip a light switch, we are not causing the light. Are just releasing what is available and ready to shine.

We believe in darkness because we have not yet centered ourselves in the power of our own BEING. As Shakespeare put it, "To be or not to be, that is the question."

Ask yourself about this: How is it possible for us to create subjectively such a complete and amazing world, which fully coordinates with equally amazing worlds others have created for themselves? How is it that every part of our world, even our mistakes and silliness, are somehow substantiated by a much larger reality that responds to our every creation; even if at times it requires some correction or amendments? Have you ever wondered how you can envision or desire something from within your personal and subjective world and then receive it or have it supplied by someone you have never seen or dreamed of before?

The answer is that light provides a constant and common communication system for everything in this universe. It carries wishes, intentions, and prayers as if they were sent on a telephone line. It connects and transmits messages to all parts of existence ranging from energy waves and particles to the complex forms of suns and galaxies. This integrated medium of communication is composed of countless filaments or strands of light that move through and connect all dimensions of existence. The matrix of light is the constant that contains, unites, and adapts each of our personal creations into a larger range of possibilities.

We are living Souls existing potentially far beyond the physical we now see! We have intrinsic ability and powers of communication far beyond our typically limited channels for connection and influence. You and I are pure energy-light in its most beautiful and intelligent configuration. If you could see yourself under a powerful electron microscope and conduct other experiments on yourself, you would see that you are made up of clusters of ever-changing particles in the form of electrons, neutrons, photons and so on.

We will not and cannot bring to light that which we are not willing to BE. Whatever we have done or thought, which we cannot also BE, will linger in the shadows. This is because light **is Being,** and **Being is light**! When Jesus said to take our light out from under the basket, he meant to stop defining our lives by negative actions that we hide, and ego pretenses that we show. Instead, we must BE our life! BE the answers we would like to find, and the changes we would like to see in the world.

Again as we were confronted with the true source and meaning of Love, we had to accept that its essential nature is a noun. God IS TRUTH. At the core of your being YOU also are the truth of your life. We have difficulty with that because of the very rich and complex conditions of reality. But even with reality, most of our limited perceptions are due to space-time curvature.

Because of space-time curvature, even literally of the earth, we can never see too far down the road. If you look out over a large flat field on a clear day, you can see for a few miles until the horizon presents a boundary. The earth has curved out of sight. If you climb a tower, its greater elevation will provide a longer angle of vision and you can see a few miles beyond the first horizon. From a helicopter or airplane, your angle of vision increases with every degree of altitude. Even from the moon, which removes all earth-bound horizons, there is the back side of the earth that can only be revealed as it spins on its axis.

There is no environment or circumstance unaffected by space-time curvature. What does this have to do with truth and spiritual mastery? A lot, actually, and rarely understood. Most of the time, we are thrown off-course by curves we did not expect. It could be a curve in the road, a curve in our health, our partnerships, in the economy, or by any sudden loss. Ideally, we will be forewarned of approaching curves, and be able to make informed corrections from a greater angle of vision. But, unfortunately, that doesn't always happen.

This space-time curvature does not happen for God, and so in his glorious wisdom is a reconciliation of truth and reality. By rising to a greater height of Being we connect with the One who personifies truth.

By envisioning what is possible, responding by instinct to opportunities that arise, and riding the great waves of life moving us forward, we can attune ourselves to revelations available within any concurrence of events. To find that special place within, where the boundaries drop between inner and outer awareness is the mystical work of each human life. In this place there is knowledge beyond what is supplied by common information. This is knowledge that sees what is possible by accessing what has always been so. Even when we cannot find truth in the world, we can each receive it as something that always was, and always will be, our indelible connection with God.

As you read this chapter, I suggest that you have a notebook that you can draw in. Make some diagrams for yourself about the cycles of communication from perfect communion to cause and effect. Find examples of how communication has progressed in your own relationships. Then create another chart showing the stages of compression, from the attraction of love, to perfect transparent overlay, into harmonious densities and finally (at times) into heavy conflicting densities. Think of such progressions that you have witnessed. As you illustrate compression with real life examples then you will remove the mystery and difficulty in understanding it. But, let's don't leave it on a sad note. Also find examples of compression where you were able to do so much more with less time and energy because you were in perfect harmony with what you were doing. The winds of grace were with you.

For your reference I have included here a larger version of the chart of creation in this chapter of Love Without End. As you read this lesson and use it to better understand the chapter, think on these things as the basic building blocks of God's reality.

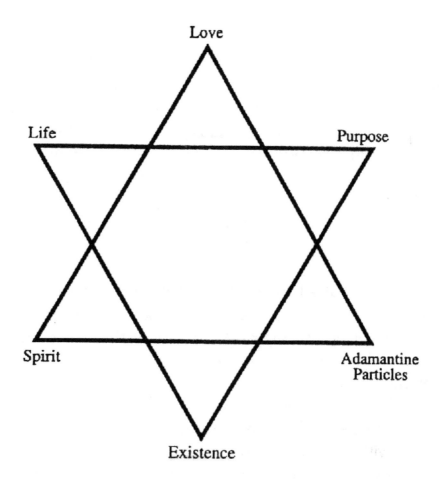

Love

Life   Purpose

Spirit   Adamantine
                        Particles

Existence

Study Questions:

1. What is the necessary relationship between our life challenges and the building of faith and consciousness?
2. What does Jesus mean by "truth is a constant?"
3. How can truth be found in both logic and miracles?
4. How does our experience of simultaneity give us a taste or remembrance of the original state of existence?
5. What are the three main types of interaction?
6. What are the three principle levels of communication?
7. How can you know the difference between illusion and reality?
8. Why does specialization deplete our energy?
9. How can harmonious compression be used to increase our production?

Study Exercises:

1. Jesus says that we are blocking our pathway to miracles by 1) dependency on structure, and 2) by trying to reshape existence to match our own illusions. Since it is often difficult to see this tendency in our own life, look at the lives of others you have known and find examples of how this has worked. Then after you feel very confident with your observations, and if you are in a healthy state of surrender from your defenses, look at how this has worked in your own life.

2. Jesus says that all three levels of communication (synchronicity, mutuality, and cause and effect) can exist concurrently in the same situation. Find at least one example of this and then examine it closely until you see that you had a choice of which level of communication you focused on.

3. Give examples of how you have used compression to do so much more with less time and energy because you were in perfect harmony with what you were doing. Then, locate instances when circumstances compressed on you because you allowed yourself to become locked in issues of conflict, or at least cause and effect (who did what to whom). With what you know now, how could you have improved those situations?

4. Find at least one example in your own life where you began with an illusion (dream, desire, or idea) and turned it successfully into reality. Find at least one example in your own life where you had to abandon an illusion that was incompatible with reality, and the cost of forcing it was not worth the effort. Now look at the difference between the first and second types of examples. What accounted for the success of the first and your need to abandon the second. You might refer back to my story of the vineyard in Paradise, Texas. How can you learn from this to make your future creative efforts more "cost efficient" and successful?

5. Simultaneously you are everything you have ever been, and also within you is a seed of everything you will ever be. Enter a meditation or prayer in which you give thanks for all your experiences, past, present, and future. Look for the "constant" within all those experiences until you are able to see the "you of you" being the central theme of it all. See how you are the constant that remains unchanged by it all and yet enhanced by the wisdom of all you have experienced.

My Personal Notes and Comments

Lesson 13

Jesus on Science

"In the depths of space,
There isn't a trace,
Of the power that brought it to be.
But it cannot hide,
If you look inside,
It was the Spirit of Life set free."
(Anonymous)

For some people science can seem overwhelming, or at least incompatible with the softer gentler faculties that we use for spiritual life and intuitive pursuits. However, it doesn't have to be that way. Science is simply the reliable standards we use for exploring the universe, and the methods we employ to make life workable in a predictable way. It can also include disciplines of study and exploration which serve to that end. Perhaps that is overly simplistic, but my objective here is to help you see that science does not require advanced education in mathematics or engineering to be relevant to your life. We are all scientists when we choose to explore how and why things work and then apply our findings to the betterment of life. How far we choose to carry that orientation of study into theoretical and technical disciplines is a personal choice and commitment.

However we do it, we are all responsible for making our lives work. This chapter was written to help us in that goal. It was written for people who want to appreciate the scientific nature of our universe in a way that is relevant to our personal experience. There are only a very few technical passages in Chapter 13. For the most part, this lesson will focus on the universal threads of science that reveal the wondrous nature of our common existence.

Contrary to common assumptions, there is no breach between science and spirituality. Jesus taught science and spirituality in the same breath. At their best, both are directed toward making life not only bearable, and workable, but also more wonderful. Spirituality offers us greater understanding and access to the realms of life not yet manifest, and science gives us understanding of that which is already in manifest form. Together, they provide us with the entire gamut of possibilities... rendered accessible, at least to our love and spirit, if not to our intellect or experience.

In the following statement, you can see the deep correlation between science and spirituality in the landscape of his thinking. They are both only as valid as the truth they embrace, reveal, or confirm:

"Truth is the breadth and depth of consciousness which transcends reality and distills it into simple understanding! It is truth that sets you free from the limiting aspects of external dependencies and conditions. Though truth is constant, its constancy must be confirmed through experience. Therefore, every man's path to transcendent awareness will be unique. Truth has its roots in a common reality, yet it is not archetypal. You see,

truth is not separate from the reality it serves. It is indigenous to it. God is not separate from sacred truth, nor is the universe separate from its own, nor I from mine, nor you from yours. Respecting that principle of ultimate integrity is respect for truth. It is the long practice of human dishonesty that has made you think that truth is somewhere else, or enshrined in a prior domain of perfect order. Truth is a living part of existence, the constant reminder of meaning, certainty and purpose which is your compass for navigating. If one would seek to gain freedom from truth, perhaps it would first be wise to grant freedom to it!"

Regarding scientific procedure, he said, *"Reality is where you start. Truth is what you distill through observing patterns of constancy. Truth is the consummation of understanding which has proven to be workable, useful, and progressive toward life."*

Notice, as he continues his teaching about truth, he established the exact place where we can find it in our own being. It may be fruitful and enlightening to compare that statement with what you have previously studied in "The Heart is Your Higher Intelligence" and then the chapter you just finished on "God and Reality."

"The ultimate condition of truth is the point where the inner and the outer are one. No matter how completely you have studied and observed the external factors of a situation, until you have located the internally motivating forces, and their relation to the external, you do not know the complete truth. By corollary, no matter how well you understand the internal; you do not have the complete truth until you also understand its impact upon the external. The universe is implicitly and explicitly of one piece. At the point of perfect stasis between the implicit and the explicit, there is a condition of hyper synchronicity, where matter, energy, space

and time move into a 'no-resistance' mode of infinite potential. This is not the collapsing of matter. This is the synchronizing of it to a 'zero point' of perfect stasis."

There are two more extremely powerful statements he made that open gateways for exploring our own life and consciousness. The first has to do with how love defines itself and engages with itself in reflective communion. Thereby love's own identity is confirmed, and also the basis for communing with all other forms of love is established. Thus, love can be itself and love beyond itself.

"This primal power of love has within it a function of 'self-awareness,' 'self-acknowledgment,' and 'self-dialogue.' This is true regardless of whether you are referring to love as beingness or as energy. You might call it the 'I AM' force. Through internalized communion, the whole becomes aware of its variable possibilities. Differences of potential are established and activation of them begins. Simultaneously, there is a holding and a releasing action that isolates the presence of a static field, a constant existing in neutrality toward the activating variables. This field can be seen to functionally operate as the "zero point" for compressing and expanding energy. The outer perimeter of a whole can never be determined for there is no point at which one element does not connect with yet another. A whole is designated by its character and quality--not by its boundaries!"

In that statement we find the key to how love can take on unique self-defining forms and also be connected with all of life. I want to draw a further connection between that statement and another one he made a few pages later in regard to infinity.

"Infinity is the simultaneous transmission of potential through similarities of quality." Personally, I believe this is a subtle revelation about

124

the formula of immortality. Let's assume that love is a quality, most likely the ultimate quality. So, look at that statement again and notice that the simultaneous transmission (perfect compression) of potential (life) through similarities of Love = infinity. In Chapter 12 he said that all of creation begins in a state of perfect compression and perfect communion under the supervision of love and that all will eventually return to that state after its full potential has been revealed through expansion and felt a need to return to original equilibrium."

As for scientifically handling life with love let's look at another recipe:

"Once it is understood that energy is a potential comprised of a quantity, a constant, and a quality, then a formula will be developed which can be applied to many situations within and beyond the conservational field. With that understanding, conditions of infinity will be comprehensible."

This suggests that we can bring infinite possibilities into our daily life. By following that formula, we could see that in our everyday life the constant would be some truth or a reliable pre-existing reality, a "given" with which we must work. The quantity might be anything from time to resources. The quality could be love in its many forms, enthusiasm, ability, devotion, or aesthetic perception (to name a few). Through this formula, we can exactly estimate results whether we are working, studying, or creating a new relationship.

What amazes me is how scientific love really is! ...and for all that, no less sweet!

In studying this chapter, perhaps more than any other, be alert for opportunities to compare related messages in other chapters. That way you will not be overwhelmed by the technical information and be able to carry his messages into a greater comprehension of life. Remember all of

Jesus' teachings are about life, whether physical, spiritual, or eternal. The miracle of our universe is simply that it IS LIFE, which is love in action, LOVE MADE MANIFEST.

More than any other chapter, the study questions and exercises here need to accompany your progress in the main chapter of *"Love Without End,"* or even follow one complete reading of it.

Study Questions:

1. What does Jesus' mean when he indicates that truth has often been regarded as an archetypal ideal, which ordinary reality can never equal? How has that kept us from perceptions of truth available within reality? How does innocent perception work to remedy this problem?

2. What is a fixed idea?   Give one example, and how it would impair intelligence.

3. How does hyper-synchronicity relate to perfect compression and communion?

4. Why is hyper-synchronicity impossible to see without experiencing it?

5. What does Jesus mean when he says that the solution to problems must be subject-specific to the cause?

6. What allows qualities to be translated to quantity and quantities to be translated to qualities?

7. What is a panacea?

8. What is the pitfall of all panaceas?

9. What is the difference between knowing about God and knowing God as a living vital Force within life? How does this

explain why so many people become dependent on religion (all religions) never knowing God?

10. How would you have compassion for others who make the mistake in question 9, and also suggest some improvement that would be meaningful?

Study Exercises:

1. Give an example of how innocent perception gave you the answer to a problem that otherwise might have been very complicated.

2. If the purpose of science is to verify reality and not to prove theory, then we are all scientists to some degree. Give three examples of how you have used common sense, clear thinking, and innocent perception to make life work better.

3. Jesus says that the ultimate condition of truth is where the inner and the outer are one. Find examples in your life or that you have witnessed. Where is that point located within each person?

4. Explain how the Universal Mind is inherently protected from the duality of the ordinary mind.

5. Jesus said that a "whole" is marked by its character and quality not by its boundaries. He said further that the center of the whole can be marked by '0'. Write a short essay on how the Sacred Heart defines and protects your wholeness and how you do not need all the boundaries you have put up as defensive protection.

6. "There is a key to the universe. All the answers are right in front of you. Its secrets are unlocked by formulating your question. Without the right question, the answer is invisible. Therefore, approach reality with a humble, inquiring mind, open in heart and

perception, and free of judgment. If you will ask the right questions, all will be revealed!" Think about something you would really like to know. However, instead of focusing on the answer and where to find it, refine the question until the answer is either revealed or else an arrow is straightly pointing to where you can find it.

7. "True intelligence is innately humble--not in a self-effacing way-- but in the way of innocent perception and workable discernments of reality. The issues of life are like broken points in a circle of wholeness. They are very specific in nature and can be repaired only with correct assessment. There are no magic circles that descend in polite generalities and repair problems without exposure and clarification of them. Nor can you handle one problem by polishing something else which was not broken. If the foundation of a house is cracked, you are not going to fix it with a new roof or camouflage it with landscaping. The same is true of broken relationships, broken plans, and broken hearts. Find out where the break really occurred. Fix it there." Locate a persistent problem in your life and look at how you are avoiding it by looking elsewhere for the fix.

8. Look for anything in your life that you have used as a panacea (one fix for everything) whether it might be sweets, vitamins, patience, speculation, aloofness, independence, privacy, medication, or whatever. (Just think of the Middle Ages when blood-letting was a panacea not only for illness but even for depression! By the way, this is how George Washington was killed.) As you can see from this short list, any one of these items could be positive and beneficial if applied to life in an appropriate way. Applied indiscriminately to everything as if it was a magic eraser is the opposite of intelligence. Don't be embarrassed to find these habitual patterns posing as a solution, for we all have them. We must be constantly self-alert and vigilant. The important thing is to

learn the correct scientific method for living, solving problems, and enhancing our life experience.

The correct method will be subject-specific in the way it fixes the broken links of life or create new better ones. For example, contribute to what you want more of. Fix that which is broken, where it is broken. If your diet is poor, improve it, but don't expect that more exercise, vitamins, or rest will do just as well. If your performance or production is not up to par, get advice from an expert in your field, don't just take another motivational course at the library. If the grass is dying, don't automatically assume it needs more water or blame it on the dog. It could be the wrong grass for your soil or available light, or perhaps parasites. Ask a nurseryman. In general, ask yourself and life the right questions so that the real answers emerge and then address those answers in a subject-specific way. This is the scientific method for everyday life.

Now, find a panacea of some sort in your life. It doesn't have to be a big one. Identify it correctly by asking questions about what the problem really is, what you are actually trying to understand, correct, or enhance. For example, when stress would build up for my dad he would go work on the yard. It didn't fix the problem but we had the prettiest year in town. My mother would bake. I guess these two had a kind of harmony, since my dad would look forward to some pie or cake after doing the yard. But neither ritual relieved the source of stress.

Our lives will substantially improve when we learn to really observe and dissect the problem into its particulars and spend our time and energy on making progress toward a real solution. Respect the power of asking questions. Ask until the generality begins to break down and you see the specifics of what you really need to know, fix, or improve. Now formulate real solutions corresponding to these new and better answers.

Meditation:

Sit in a comfortable position, and close your eyes. Allow your body to relax as you move your attention through it from the tips of your toes to the top of your head. Shake your shoulders or roll your head if necessary. Once you are physically relaxed, tell your mind to relax. Draw your attention gently into the area of your heart by deepening your breath. As you inhale, allow your abdomen to swell and hold the breath for as long as you can. Exhale slowly and experience the cleansing release. Feel the seamless unity between your inner and outer worlds. Within this unity, find the center point that is the heart of your being.

Breathe and focus on this center until you see a point of light. As you continue to breathe, fan the spark and see it grow. See it light up your physical heart and begin to enter the blood stream and flow throughout your body. Follow the light through the arteries to every limb, every organ, and every cell. Then see the light return to its source in the heart. Now see these cells form a common light around the outer skin of your body. Notice how it touches the air, lighting the room or landscape where you are until it reaches the walls or distant horizon. Send this light through the rivers of the earth as you did the arteries of your body. See the light empty into the oceans and reach seamlessly from sea to sea. Behold the light of the rivers and oceans becoming a common light that encircles the earth. Now see the lighted atmosphere touch the magnetic space between earth and sun. The two lights are joined and become a common light throughout the solar system. As this happens, imagine our solar system to be a dot of light in the heavens. Fan it with your breath, as you did the light of your heart, until it unites with the light of other stars. The galaxy is now one light that joins with the light of other galaxies. Wherever you see an outer edge to light, see it touch and expand into the next element until there is no separation. If you encounter any holes of darkness, see them filled with light as a waterfall fills a stream. Expand this perception until there is seamless light throughout the universe.

Dwell in the glorious presence of endless light, total possibility, and perfect love. Behold: your inner world! God has given it to you as a mirror of the outer world, so that you may also share the experience of creation, imagination, choice, freedom, love, and pure being. In this light, see your life as it has been. Now see your life as it can be.

With your eyes still closed, begin to make connections between the inner and outer worlds. First, notice the texture of your breath and the temperature of your environment. Then notice the feeling of gravity beneath your body. With your hand, touch something around you and begin to move your limbs. Finally, open your eyes. The first thing that will catch your attention is light. Focus with love upon it and remember the sacred connection in your heart.

Prayer

Divine Creator of all beings, of all worlds, of all times,
Fire of the Spirit and life within us,
We pray that your light stream forth into the minds of men
And descend upon the earth.
We pray that your love stream forth into the hearts of men
And descend upon the earth.
We pray that your grace stream forth into the lives of men
And descend upon the earth.
We rejoice in these gifts and offer our homage, love, and faith.
Amen

My Personal Notes and Comments

Lesson 14

Pathways to Success

"Will you not open your hearts to know
What rainbows teach and sunsets show!"
Ralph Waldo Emerson

"You are here to learn the process through which sacred transformation occurs in all times and places. The raw material of Planet Earth is fertile ground for demonstrating to the children of God an eternal truth: as the internal is fulfilled, the external is brought into alignment and manifestation. Likewise, as the external is created according to the will of God, the internal reclaims its original perfection. You were created in the likeness of God to extend the creative powers of our Father into all the dimensions in which you dwell, seek, and create. Where you are is where your work unfolds. You are where you were meant to be."

In this opening quote from Chapter 14, we are essentially told that success does not lie somewhere else. It happens naturally from within ourselves, as we unfold our true potential in relation to the laws of the universe. This is level of success is sustainable, unlike the fickle vicissitudes of good or bad fortune that result from more competitive approaches to accomplishment.

In this chapter he gives us four principles of success that always work. The beauty of these four principles is how intertwined they are. As you practice one, all the others are activated to some degree. As you practice them all, the whole of your life rises to a different octave. The next thing to seek is truth with a tolerant attitude toward other's and their perception or experience of truth.

The next most pivotal paragraph of this chapter addresses the universality of truth, which still honors our own perceptions of it:

> *"The miracle of truth is that it is unique for each and yet constant for all. This relates to another principle which is crucial to alignment with our Father's will, and that is the law of mutuality. Mutuality allows expansion and differences to occur in the universe or among humankind without loss of harmony. All communication is based upon this law of mutuality. If there were no mutuality between two people, there would be no sense in talking. Neither person could understand the other. However, without different experiences or viewpoints to share, what would be the point of communicating? On the very obvious level, having a common language is mutuality. Through a common language, differences may be compared and overcome, if necessary. Through mutual understanding you are set free from another's viewpoint. You do not have to serve the dreams of another. All you have to do is honor the other person's right to dream, for in honoring his right, you honor your own. This is the blessing of mutuality."*

Truth assures our greater good within the whole of things. It is carried by the will of God and functions in harmony with love, which is the energy of all creation. Therefore, it is a power we must respect if we are to enjoy lasting success. When our success is aligned with truth it has more constancy.

"Will" is the other power we must understand if we are to arrive at a truly successful life. This can be a difficult concept for most of us because we have so many associations between will, willfulness, and dominance. Almost everyone has had an experience of being overridden by someone else's stronger will or desire. Most likely this began in childhood with our parents, who denied us something that was probably for our own good...but we did not see it that way at the time. As we learn and grow, we begin to accept that there are many more levels of will at play in our life than our own. Jesus described how the various levels of will unfold and how each must be reconciled to our own will if we are to make much progress on the highway of life.

Free will is a very misunderstood idea. Too often it is regarded as a license to be irresponsible and childish. We have all been given free will, but that is not so much the freedom to do any silly or destructive thing we wish (although many have used it that way). It is really the freedom to choose how we navigate the 'rivers of will', which includes every prevalent force from God's will to the will of others. When we understand this river of will, then we can make educated choices about how to navigate it and travel on it toward our greatest good with an over-all benefit for others. Freedom is really the gift of understanding and the opportunity of applying it to life so that you may experience the fullness of life uniquely, in your own way, gaining the ultimate experience of the inner and outer life being one.

With this formula, success is assured. What it will look like externally is always unique, because it takes its power from the way you are and how completely you have evolved yourself in relation to the universe, to others, and to God.

Study questions:

1. What are the four principles of success?
2. What is the main reason most people are stuck with the 'dead and the dying'?
3. What is the intelligence of forgiving to which Jesus referred?
4. What are the four levels of intent?
5. What is a viewpoint of reality?

6. Does your viewpoint of reality create a desirable place for you, for others, and for God?

Study exercises:

1. Give examples in your own life of how the four principles of success have worked, and how, to the contrary, you invited unnecessary problems when you did not apply them.

2. Practice forgiveness and observe how it returns you to 'life and the living.' Then inventory all the points of grievance and hurt that you have not forgiven and notice how it tacks you to the past. Is it worth it? Consider what might happen if you just let go.

3. Describe the harmony between intelligence and forgiving and the harmony between creativity and forgiving.

4. The four levels of intent exist in any situation. Pick any situation in your life and write a sentence or two describing the four levels of intent in that situation. Then write a summary sentence or two about how you could increase your effectiveness in that situation by establishing a greater harmony between all four levels. Some you must simply accept, some you may negotiate, and some you may change. Knowing the difference and acting accordingly to bring greater positive focus can enhance your life measurably.

5. Notice how your personal reality and your viewpoints of reality can either create or deny a positive place for your self and others. You can even create the illusion of God being absent from your life by disallowing space in which He is acknowledged.

    Armed with that knowledge, create a place for everything, every project, or desire that you want in your life. To create a place for your desire is the most affirming action you can take, even if it only happens in your mind's eye. An example of this is the extremely high percentage of parents who were not able to conceive a child, then could (and did) do so in the few months after first adopting a child. The adopted child created a place for children in their life. Previously, the omission of that place within their life (for whatever reason) was so great that it resulted in infertility. The same is true for creation or growth of anything. If you put two persons side by side in a race to rise above conditions of poverty, the one who will most likely win is the one who observed and used natural forms of wealth around him.

Therefore, in this exercise, you will be doing a "dress rehearsal" for something that is important to you. Let's say you want to make a contribution in your community.

First, get a clear concept of your goal and desired result. Next, think of the people with whom you will share either the goal or its result. Do this as a stage design. Give it actual space, such as places where you will meet, or maybe the courthouse where you will file a petition, or a Mayor's office, or land to which lumber and bricks will be delivered.

Next, see how this project either extends or displaces the spaces you now live in or frequently visit. In other words, unite it with the spaces you already create or give it permission to replace or extend them.

> Not wanting to give up what we already have is often a big hurdle to moving into something new. So, you must resolve any possible conflicts there.

Last, see the **qualities** that are in your envisioned space and the qualities, such as enthusiasm, which you are bringing to it. Affirm that it is in fact a worthy project to bring about (do the right thing). Allow it to be infused with life and the living. And, hold it as the love that you are. It will come to life.

When we follow the four principles of success with complete honesty and unreserved devotion, also remembering to create a place for it within our perceptions of reality, it will come true.

Meditation

Your meditation for this chapter is taken from *"The Keys of Jeshua,"* Chapter 22, "Restoring the Temple." There is a great relationship between the ability to be successful in living and being in your personal temple, alive with integrity and meaning.

Your life is your temple, and within that great temple are many specialized temples. To varying degrees, these may be broken temples. Columns are standing tall in some temples, and shattered in others. Some passageways are open and some have collapsed. Some temples are full of song, and others are haunted with the memory of dreams that were lost or abandoned. Some temples you cannot bear to enter because you cannot forgive.

The purpose of this meditation is to draw all parts of your life into a single, unified whole. It is all right and appropriate to keep whatever feelings are currently associated with the parts and passages of your life. You cannot recreate a meaningful whole with dishonest feelings about the former events. Some of the parts will be full of joy and excitement, and some may be full of anger or grief. Other parts you would rather not look at again. I assure you that they do not go away simply because you do not accept them. The place to start is with the way things really are.

Be seated in a comfortable chair, close your eyes, and breathe easily without effort or forced attention. Relax your body and release the tension of the day. To help this along, start with your toes. Wiggle them and move your feet until they are free of tension. Move up to your ankles, and gently rotate them until you can begin to feel the relaxation move up through your legs. Continue upward into your lower body.

138

Consider each body part as special, and acknowledge its membership in the whole. Take this opportunity to show each part of your body its membership in the whole and express your gratitude for what it does. If there is any pain, discomfort, sickness, or dysfunction, notice the feeling in that organ or body part and acknowledge that feeling as part of the whole no matter what it is. No part suffers alone. Continue moving up through your body to the top of your head and your scalp. Squint your eyes and release them. Repeat this several times to relax your scalp and the muscles of your face.

Now sink into relaxation and focus on your breath. This is the breath of your life.

Imagine that you are sitting inside an enormous, clear bubble and the walls of the bubble reflect back to you the events of your life. Find a place on the walls of the bubble for every part of your life for every joy, hope, duty, triumph, disappointment, boring endurance, and exciting adventure. Find a place for every exquisite feeling, every sickness, every loss, and every moment of happiness.

With every breath, inhale into your consciousness whatever memory is available for you to examine. There is no order of importance, because everything has a place in the whole of your life. Not everything is available at one time, and this meditation is something you can repeat throughout your life. Therefore, patience and acceptance are crucial attitudes as you proceed into this examination of your temple.

The most important thing is to accept each memory, incident, or event that comes forth as YOUR experience. See and feel what was really happening for YOU! Look at every sensation, every opinion, and every conclusion you made about this incident at the time it happened. Now look to see if there were also feelings, opinions, beliefs, or decisions, which were NOT yours, which had an influence on the way you responded. Exhale with gusto, and release everything that was not yours. See the energy of others dissolve into particles that blow away. Carefully place the part of the memory that was truly yours back on the inner wall of your bubble. Know that it will be there for all time, but it may now take on a different order of importance or a different meaning as your own true experience.

Repeat this as many times as your interest and energy can be vitally engaged with the process. When you begin to feel a sense of completion and restoration you have accomplished enough for one day. Before you end, survey the inner wall of the bubble and notice if any new alignments have happened. Perhaps it is now lighter and more sparkling, or more resilient and flexible. What makes the walls of your temple hard, brittle, and breakable are elements that are not truly your own. These elements are the contributions of others that you have held onto out of vanity, misunderstanding, confusion, or lack of forgiveness.

As you restore the pillars of your temple, you will notice the progress first by a greater sense of innocence and a willingness to see and accept your experiences exactly as they were without judgment or false coloring. As your acceptance increases, forgiveness will become easier, and you will find it possible to retain the memory of events and people, while forgiving the hurt and disappointments connected with them. That will be the hardest part of your progress. After that, you will find more and more peace as you clean and restore the pieces of your temple. Wisdom will come as you begin to take the restored pieces and find new meaning and new patterns of integration. It will be as if you have taken on a new life. Your heart will begin to fill with the miracle of a restored temple and you will behold the amazing abundance of all you have lived and experienced. Joy will fill every part of your being. From this place of fulfillment, compassion will take on a new meaning as you look around at the world and all those with whom you share life. There will be love, tolerance, true understanding, and reverence for the presence of Christ in your life, pouring through you to others. These are the feelings and benchmarks that you will recognize as you restore the temple of your life.

Prayer

Gracious Creator
Be with me as I learn the great lessons of life.
Teach me to cherish my experiences
For the grace and intelligence they bring to my heart,
For the sharing they give me with others,
For the richness they bring to my life,
For the certainty they demonstrate of your love.
Give me the courage to release my attachments to story
Like a cup returning its water to a flowing river,
And in that moment
Show to me the true meaning of reunion.

Amen

My Personal Notes and Comments

Lesson 15

The Beloved

This last chapter of *"Love Without End"* is not only the culminating message but also it is a summary of every other major concept in the book. In this chapter we are able to see all the topica discussed earlier, including reality, perception, faith, consciousness, judgment, and separation, finally addressed together as conditions of BEING and how our being relates to our Source.

Life is its own sacred essence that extends well past the containers we use for accessing it and claiming it to be our own. The key to a fuller, richer life rests in knowing that life is the vital force that exists beyond all other contexts. It is life that restores health, and not health that restores life. The ultimate realization is that life is available beyond all physical form and is not lost just because physical forms may perish.

As the Apostle Paul said, we are one person; we are one body with many parts. I believe we will not find all the answers to life or the fullness of it until we reach out and become the other parts of our self and witness life in its greater perspective and potential.

The soul makes one of many. It is the great container of infinite contexts. It holds together all the many ways of being you. It holds all the beginnings, middles and ends of you. It holds all the emotions and feelings, ideas and ideals, desires and disappointments, intentions and avoidances. It holds the doorways to the earthly and the spiritual. The soul is where your biography and biology meet in space and time to collaborate on your eternal divinity.

A tiny magnet in the soul holds everything as one. It is a word. That word is "I." It is not quite a name but it is your soul's identity. You have a given name that marks your place in the world. You have lots of other names in space and time that signify different parts of you; your life, relationships, or work. "I" is the only signifier of all of you at all times in all ways. "I" is the unity of your individuality. This seems to be consistent with all the definitions of life.

There is another unity dwelling in our souls. It is our humanity. Our humanity unifies each one with everyone who has ever existed or ever will exist in time and space. All the people we know and don't know, those we like and don't like, those who believe in the same God as we do and those who's gods have other names. Our humanity is the soul that mirrors the sun shining on all of us throughout time. It is the other side of the unity coin in our soul, the universal experience of being human.

The unity coin is always being flipped. When you breathe in the coin flips to your individuality. When you breathe out it flips to your humanity. When you speak it flips to your individuality. When you listen it flips to your humanity.

It is about this endless phenomenon that Jesus spoke of our ego and how it fixates us on one side of the coin. The fact is we all need a center for attracting and holding the desires of our life. When we forget (or perhaps never have considered) that love is who we really are, a person will center on the most productive substitute he can find. In addition to being a distortion of the truth, the greatest problem with substitute identities is that they do not allow us to find our place in a larger unity. This is why we commonly use the term "egotistical" to denote those people who set themselves apart from others, in a typically pretentious and protective way.

When we are conscious, however, and wise to the duality of our unity, life's journey reflects multi-dimensional love. With consciousness we can take the coin of unity and stand it on its side. Then we can take "unity" out of the horizontal and into a vertical plane that reflects the soul as the bridge between spirit and matter. Now, give unity a spin. We all know that a flat circular coin spinning on its side looks like a sphere.

As a "sphere" our souls express the unity that exists between the self, the other, the spiritual and the earthly. When it spins fast enough the sphere becomes virtually transparent, one side dissolving into the other.

When we contemplate unity, it is easier to bring all the systems of our life into balance. Were it not for all of life, the smallest part of life would not be possible. The smallest part of life can, and does, influence the whole. All of life is connected through its common elements and extended matrix. Whether you are referring to organic life of Earth or life of the cosmos, it always occurs in a context with other life, in unison with other life forms. Life is a property of whole systems, not of any individual organism. Life is assured because it is the summation of three eternal elements: Love, Spirit, and the Adamantine Particles — the essence of creation — the presence of the Creator.

The entirety of Jesus' presence in the world, then and now is to teach us how to have a better life. We flippantly, or casually, speak about quality of life as if it were a commodity such as a better home or car. Rarely do we focus on the love, life, and higher consciousness that really provide our quality of life.

All of "Love Without End" is about directing us toward a bank account of fresh energy with which to renew and expand our lives. We know it must be somewhere, because in spite of the fact that the structural arrangements of our universe are conservatively fixed, the universe is also dynamically expanding! Actually, reserves of energy are everywhere, in patterned form and in unpatterned free flow. Life is both. It is unique in every configuration, like rare and precious snowflakes, and yet connected, pattern to pattern, with the whole of existence. It is all around us, in everything, free for the taking, and yet we are starving because we do not know how to take it. Instead we continue plugging into power sources, such as food, work, social influence, money, competition, and then exchanging it with others for the pay it will hopefully bring.

It takes great courage and compassion to navigate the waters of life. As surely as we each have moments of joy and ecstasy, we will also have moments of challenge and grief. If all we had was a linear perspective of life, there would be no way to make sense of it all. At best, we might be able to make the scales balance, but then we would still be faced with the final question, "what's the point?" Fortunately, we have been given a 'center' to our being, and from that center we may apply values and priorities to our life experiences so that these events can be integrated into a meaningful whole. As we cultivate this center, we become more aware of who we really are and simultaneously become less affected by the events of life. We become self-defining souls, sculpting our lives not by its events but by our love, values, priorities, beliefs, and dedication.

The power of love within us is greater than anything we can currently comprehend. There are countless stories of heroic accomplishments and miraculous feats that have demonstrated the power of love in everyday living. But, as we have all learned by now, it is not just a feeling or an action. Love is who we are. That is where all of our loving actions take their root.

Jesus came to Earth to ignite the living fire of "The Beloved" within each of us. Saint Paul was the first to comprehend the profundity of that concept, and with this understanding he formulated a message that changed the world. He saw that worship without love is a meaningless formality devoid of any intrinsic purpose or value. Worship is often misdirected. But, adoration is not. That extremely high and pure emotion seems to be exempt from the perils of vanity as well as the structures of ritual. Within that profound feeling we have a connection between our self and Divinity, regardless of the context in which we acknowledge the presence of God. Adoration refines and renews the purity of our own spirit and brings us back into being who we really are.

Since the ability to center and integrate is indigenous to all humans, I believe that everyone is to some degree aware of its value to their lives. There comes a time, however, in the lives of those who are ready, when awareness of this center accelerates to the point that it is not just the basis for integrating life, but also for commanding life, making choices, and creating new and better avenues of experience. It is at such moments that we understand HOW LOVED WE HAVE ALWAYS BEEN. And that LOVE is WHO we are!

Regardless of how far we drifted into the adventure of life, this sacred center has always been preserved at the core of our being, to be ready for our eventual journey home. This is the moment when we enter Christ Consciousness, and begin to seek our life simply as an extension of the love that we are. Regardless of our challenges or how far we had drifted out to sea, all our desires are now guided only by the 'north star' of this new and higher realization.

It is a paradox that in this sacred center we have the greatest sense of our personal uniqueness and also have more access to unity than from any other reference point in consciousness. Perhaps it is because, here, we are most like God. Whatever the reasons, all of which would fall short of the Great Mystery, in this place we also know The Beloved, the unified spirit of Love in harmony with all creation.

To this end, *"Love Without End"* was written, and for the purpose of taking your study of it to a higher level of Christ Consciousness, this course was prepared. While you are reading this chapter, think back to all the earlier chapters, and review them in your heart from this higher centering in Love.

Pierre Tielhard De Chardin, the great philosopher priest of the twentieth century said it so beautifully: "The day will come when, after harnessing space, the winds, the tides, and gravitation, we shall harness for God the energies of Love. And on that day, for the second time in the history of the world, we shall have discovered fire.

For me, that is what "The Beloved" really means.

Study Questions:

1. Why is laughter so important in regaining our love?
2. What is ego?
3. What did Jesus mean when he said a man must give up his life to find it?
4. Why does the ego feed on fear when love does not?
5. What did Jesus mean by separating the sheep from the goats?
6. Why is it necessary to 'reduce' the past in order to have a more creative orientation to the future?
7. What is the difference between shaping reality and inventing it?
8. What was the original sin?
9. What did Jesus accomplish for mankind by separating as an act of love?
10. Why is free will a necessary part of personal salvation?

Study Exercises:

1. Recall an experience that gave you the feeling of adoration. Immerse yourself in that feeling and allow it to anoint your soul with a higher love.
2. Find a time in your life when to grant mercy would have defeated ego and redeemed yourself.
3. Notice times in your life when your own 'true person' showed up differently than might have been expected from your past or images you have about yourself.
4. Recall at least one 'sand castle' you had to let go of in order to have a more workable reality.
5. How can we partake in Jesus' gift?
6. Write a short essay entitled: "In our unity we are the Beloved"

Meditation:

Jesus said, "The Kingdom of Heaven is within you." Dense though our bodies may seem, they are actually mostly space, and the few densities that comprise them are condensations of light. The only other reality or context that defines our physical existence is that our bodies are also part of the genetic-biological cycle of life, with its desires, needs, perils, and pleasures. This extends into the various contexts of social living. For most of our lives, we are focused on these more complex challenges of physical life. Just imagine what might happen if we shifted our emphasis to the first aspect of space and light, which is equally physical from another perspective.

The Divine forces, which have produced your higher immortal body, are literally waiting within each cell to be released. Through deep meditation, you have an opportunity to meet the living Christ existing within and around you. He will accompany you on this journey homeward.

Now, let's discuss the pathway. From the crown of your head to the end of your spine, there are at least eight cerebrospinal centers. These are the nexus points where organic substance, energy, emotion, thought, consciousness, and spirit are joined. Where they are, what they are called, and their possible functions are probably less important than a simple awareness that they exist. Though their differences may be subtle, the elements joined at these points form the bridge between Heaven and Earth. Their union also results in certain vibrational qualities, which may be opened through visualization, activated through energy, and explored through consciousness. The master vibration is love, and the most basic perceptions are of light, color, and subtle movement.

To begin, find a comfortable chair or mat where your spine may be straight. Steady your gaze as you allow your eyes to gently close. Observe your breath and begin to softly inhale through the nostrils, relaxing the abdomen outward. This permits the diaphragm to move downward and the lungs to expand into the lower chest cavity. Hold a deep, full, inhalation for a moment and then slowly exhale through the nostrils. Repeat this until a calm state of mind and an ample supply of oxygen fill your being.

Now visualize your spinal column as being a hollow pipe. Begin using it as a breathing instrument by mentally transferring the sensation of inhaling and exhaling to it. Perceive that your breath is moving inter-dimensionally through your spine—upwardly as you inhale and downwardly as you exhale. As you inhale from the earth, imagine this gift of energy and love to be the presence of our beloved Mother God, and as you exhale, experience the cleansing release of all things temporal as you are received into the embrace of our Almighty Father God. Allow this process to continue until complete surrender has induced a rhythmic and harmonious flow of energy on all levels of consciousness. After this happens, focus your attention on the area of the heart and visualize a spark of light. See this light grow through the nurturing of God's love and your acceptance of it until it becomes a womb-like aura containing the presence of a child. Look into the eyes of this child and form a steady gaze until there is a transmission of love, recognition, and wisdom. This child is not the youngster of your human history—but the eternal soul that you are, ever young, tender, and innocent, though compassionate and wise. This is the divine child that is YOU, as seen through the eyes of God. This is the divine child who lives in the Kingdom of Heaven.

In the presence of this child, allow yourself to be accepted for all that you have been and all that you have experienced. On the flow of your soft and rhythmic breath enjoy the sweet and eternal dialogue between your original self, created in the image of God, and yourself that embarked on an adventure. LOVE as pure being is now engaged with love that is having an experience. Enjoy the pleasure of knowing thyself. Remain in the Kingdom as long as it beckons to you.

Prayer

Father Mother God,
I pray for the simplicity of being which honors all of life,
That in honoring you and all others,
I am honored as well.
I was given everything and did not know how to receive.
I did not know how to honor the blessing of life.
I asked for my needs to be met, when my only need was
To honor the power of Love.
Now, in knowing this, I rest in your peace,
Create with your infinite supply,
And exist forever in your truth.

Amen

My Personal Notes and Comments

Lesson 16

The Summation

The course has been about something more important than clarifying and absorbing information. As he has said, "If you do not become what I have taught you in your heart, then the words are to no avail." That, of course involves recognizing and accepting that as a child of Love, we too have the Christ potential in our hearts.

As my life moved on through the years, I too dealt with these same challenges. I knew after the painting project was complete; I would leave the high ground and live an ordinary life. But, I also knew that it would be a transformed kind of 'ordinary life.' I would never be the same. My new goal was to fully receive the blessings I had been given, to infuse my life with it completely, and yet be 'in the world' proceeding with the life I had chosen.

Anyone who has been touched by this book has also received a sacramental blessing of 'truth revealed.' Now the question is: "What will you do with it inside the life you have chosen?" Let us began our search, in the heart, for therein are all beginnings and endings within the cycles of our everlasting life.

You have embarked on a path of realizing and accepting the presence of The Christ within, which is your own birthright and your own original state of being. Otherwise, it could not be said that in our innocence we were created in the image of God!

Because you are a 'whole' being, and are, by extension, part of a greater 'whole', you have senses that can detect the normally unseen parts of our larger being and environment. Normally we focus on the obvious, and now you are also aware of unseen factors on other levels of consciousness. We ONLY lose this awareness to the degree that we believe in and practice separation.

The answer is faith. Faith is the measure of our commitment to overcome separation, embrace the truth of our wholeness, and live without indulging any illusions of failure, illness, or misery. Faith is the courage we have to be totally in present time, without any need for justification or reservation. When we have faith in our wholeness and the wholeness of all life, our vision is penetrating, our health radiant, our consciousness boundless, and our remembrance without flaw. Faith is a bond that holds firm our connection with all of life.

Nothing works better with our faith than an expanding consciousness, for it is faith that assures consciousness that the far horizon has treasures to explore.

Your continuing assignment:

The Beloved, which you just finished, is the culmination point of the teaching that Love is who you are, as well as the other key themes of the wondrous universe, faith, and consciousness. It also contained the recipe for overcoming ego limitations. From the viewpoint of that chapter now look back over the book using three reference points:

1.   Return to the earlier passages that were your favorites and read them again. You may now see why you liked them so much, and there may be even more revelations.

2.   Return to the earlier passages that you had the greatest difficulty with. See how this greater perspective sheds new light on what you could not see clearly before.

3.   Open the book spontaneously, and see what it now offers you.

My Personal Notes and Comments

May your life be richly blessed

Glenda Green, M.A., D.D.

Glenda Green is one of the world's leading teachers of contemporary spirituality. Her teachings revolve around universal truths that are uplifting and enlightening to all people of all beliefs. From poetry to science, her teaching moves the reader to deep waters of understanding.

Within her body of work are some of the most complete, extensive treatments of pure science ever found in spiritual literature. World-renowned scientists have conferred with Glenda about these astounding revelations.

She has authored the best-selling books, *Love Without End...Jesus Speaks, The Keys of Jeshua,* the best-selling lecture series, *Conversations With Jesus,* and the internationally acclaimed portraits of Christ, *"The Lamb and The Lion," and "Jeshua."*

In addition to her writing and teaching, she is also acknowledged by the nation's leading scholars, critics, and museum officials as one of the world's foremost realist painters and spiritual artists. Her paintings are housed in major public art collections, including the Smithsonian Institution.

She has taught on the faculties of Tulane University and the University of Oklahoma. She is an exceptional public speaker in high demand. Her warm, witty and confident manner evokes our inner certainty of a higher awareness. With a clean energetic style, and masterful comprehension of the most critical spiritual issues, she offers her readers and listeners an exceptional opportunity to acquire a truer, more complete understanding of the universe and their own place in it.

Biographical references include, *North American Women Artists of the Twentieth Century: A Biographical Dictionary,* edited by Jules Heller and Nancy G. Heller; *Angels A to Z,* by James R. Lewis and Evelyn Oliver, 1996. *Who's Who in American Art,* (15th and 16th Editions); *Who's Who in the South and Southwest,* (17th, 18th, and 19th Editions); *Who's Who of American Women* (12th, 13th, and 14th Editions); *Dictionary of International Biography,* Vol. 16;

Spiritis Book Store

Books by Glenda Green:

"Love Without End: Jesus Speaks"	$24.88
"The Keys of Jeshua"	$24.88
"The Way to a Greater Life"	$19.88
"Anointed With Oil"	$19.95

Tapes: *"Conversations With Jesus"*

Each tape is a full 90 minutes of power-packed information from the original conversations between Jeshua and Glenda Green. This was her original public release.

      14 CD album $140.00

Prayers and Meditations from "The Keys of Jeshua"

This is an audio recording of 12 prayers and meditations from *"The Keys of Jeshua"* in Glenda's voice. It begins with a powerful introduction to meditation and prayer, and is enriched throughout with deeply heart-centered music.

      2 CD album $24.95

A complete list of our products and services is available on our website
www.inspiredorigination.com

To receive our weekly online newsletter, you may sign up there as well.

Bookstores may purchase directly from us, or through most major distributors.